TRIO
READING 1

The Intersection of
Vocabulary, Critical Thinking, & Reading

Kate Adams

OXFORD

UNIVERSITY PRESS

OXFORD
UNIVERSITY PRESS

198 Madison Avenue
New York, NY 10016 USA

Great Clarendon Street, Oxford, OX2 6DP, United Kingdom

Oxford University Press is a department of the University of Oxford.
It furthers the University's objective of excellence in research, scholarship,
and education by publishing worldwide. Oxford is a registered trade
mark of Oxford University Press in the UK and in certain other countries

ISBN: 978 0 19 400078 9 STUDENT BOOK 1 WITH ONLINE PRACTICE PACK
ISBN: 978 0 19 400383 4 STUDENT BOOK 1 AS PACK COMPONENT
ISBN: 978 0 19 400386 5 ONLINE PRACTICE WEBSITE

Printed in China

This book is printed on paper from certified and well-managed sources

ACKNOWLEDGEMENTS

Cover Design: Yin Ling Wong

Illustrations by: Ben Hasler: 11, 13, 32, 36, 43, 59 (tl, tr, br), 83, 108, 112, 115;
Joe Taylor: 20, 21, 24, 44, 47, 70, 77, 96, 120, 121; 5W Infographics: 59 (bl), 63,
64, 124, 126, 127.

*The publishers would like to thank the following for their kind permission to reproduce
photographs:* M J Perris/Alamy, pg. 1 (houses); Galyna Andrushko/Shutterstock,
pg. 1 (sky); Photodisc/OUP, pg. 1 (map); Lane Oatey/Getty Images, pg. 2 (man);
imanhakim/Shutterstock, pg. 2 (pen); Pshenichka/Shutterstock/OUP, pg. 2
(book); JLP/Jose L. Pelaez/Corbis, pg. 2 (girl); studio2013/Shutterstock, pg. 2
(cup); Nina Buday/Shutterstock, pg. 2 (baby); Lane Oatey/Getty Images, pg.
5 (man); imanhakim/Shutterstock, pg. 5 (pen); Pshenichka/Shutterstock/
OUP, pg. 5 (book); Rayes/Photodisc/OUP, pg. 8 (boy); g215/Shutterstock, pg.
8 (park); studio2013/Shutterstock, pg. 8 (cup); JLP/Jose L. Pelaez/Corbis, pg.
8 (girl); Peter Steiner/Alamy, pg. 8 (school); McIek/Shutterstock, pg. 8 (map);
Radius Images/Alamy, pg. 8 (woman); Iriana Shiyan/Shutterstock, pg. 8
(home); Mike Theiss/Getty Images, pg. 8 (sun); Iriana Shiyan/Shutterstock,
pg. 8 (home); studio2013/Shutterstock, pg. 8 (cup); Radius Images/Alamy,
pg. 8 (woman); Don Mason/Getty Images, pg. 9 (girls); McIek/Shutterstock,
pg. 9 (map); M J Perris/Alamy, pg. 9 (houses); Mike Stone/OUP, pg. 9 (girl);
GrayMark/Shutterstock, pg. 9 (shirt); Peter Dazeley/Getty Images, pg. 9 (small
box); Image Source/Getty Images, pg. 9 (boys); Michael Kraus/Shutterstock,
pg. 9 (pants); Helder Almeida/Shutterstock, pg. 9 (big box); Hurst Photo/
Shutterstock, pg. 9 (men); pukach/Shutterstock, pg. 9 (socks); parinyabinsuk/
Shutterstock, pg. 9 (sad boy); Monkey Business Images/Shutterstock, pg.
9 (women); AID/amanaimages/Corbis/OUP, pg. 9 (black hair); Eri Morita/
Getty Images, pg. 9 (happy girl); Ricardo Reitmeyer/Shutterstock, pg. 10
(moon); Nina Buday/Shutterstock, pg. 10 (baby); kampolz/Shutterstock, pg.
10 (building); danishkhan/Getty Images, pg. 10 (boy); yui/Shutterstock, pg.
10 (ocean); Galyna Andrushko/Shutterstock, pg. 10 (sky); Severin Schweiger/
Getty Images, pg. 11 (girls jumping); Jose Luis Pelaez, Inc./Blend Images/
Corbis, pg. 11 (man reading); Justin Lo/Getty Images, pg. 11 (snow); Robert
Kneschke/Shutterstock, pg. 11 (student); Denis Vrublevski/Shutterstock,
pg. 12 (man listening); Peter Zelei Images/Getty Images, pg. 12 (sun rises);
manley099/Getty Images, pg. 12 (desks); Tetra Images - Rob Lewine/Getty
Images, pg. 12 (teacher); Christopher Futcher/Getty Images, pg. 12 (girl
kicking ball); age fotostock/Alamy, pg. 12 (boy running); Blend Images/

Shutterstock, pg. 19 (family); PeopleImages.com/Getty Images, pg. 19
(women); Andrew Watson/Getty Images, pg. 19 (art museum); Celso Pupo/
Shutterstock, pg. 26 (Lionel Messi); Allstar Picture Library/Alamy, pg. 28
(Lionel Messi); Carlos andre Santos/Shutterstock, pg. 33 (books); Subbotina
Anna/Shutterstock, pg. 33 (kitchen); Sebastian Duda/Shutterstock/OUP, pg.
33 (sports equipment); Kamenetskiy Konstantin/Shutterstock/OUP, pg. 33
(plane); Steve Debenport/Getty Images, pg. 39 (small talk); kristian sekulic/
Getty Images, pg. 45 (school); Guy Bell/Alamy, pg. 45 (line of people); Sophie
James/Shutterstock, pg. 45 (Burj Khalifa); Hero Images/Getty Images, pg. 45
(doctor); Free Agents Limited/Corbis, pg. 48 (Mona Lisa); Werner Forman
Archive/Bridgeman Images, pg. 51 (masks); Erik Simonsen/Getty Images,
pg. 57 (satellite); Den Rise/Shutterstock, pg. 57 (laptop); Ocean Image
Photography/Shutterstock, pg. 57 (surfer); rawmn/Shutterstock, pg. 58
(landscaping); Gabriele Maltinti/Shutterstock, pg. 58 (earth and moon);
Timothy Hodgkinson/Shutterstock, pg. 58 (earth); Vibrant Image Studio/
Shutterstock, pg. 58 (beach); Erik Simonsen/Getty Images, pg. 62 (satellite);
Petra Christen/Shutterstock, pg. 62 (penguins); 3Dsculptor/Shutterstock,
pg. 63 (satellite); swatchandsoda/Shutterstock, pg. 70 (hieroglyphs);
windmoon/Shutterstock, pg. 71 (parade); Katie Garrod/JAI/Corbis, pg. 71
(kids laughing); Lucky Business/Shutterstock, pg. 71 (people eating); John
Lund/Drew Kelly/Getty Images, pg. 70 (children playing); Simon D. Warren/
Corbis, pg. 74 (laptop and iPhone); Henry Lederer/Getty Images, pg. 82 (man
sailing); DanielBendjy/Getty Images, pg. 82 (woman in park); Pavel Ilyukhin/
Shutterstock, pg. 82 (tourist); Giovanni G/Shutterstock, pg. 82 (girl studying);
Valentin Casarsa/Getty Images, pg. 82 (woman riding bike); Travelpix
Ltd/Getty Images, pg. 82 (man taking selfie); Edd Westmacott/Alamy,
pg. 86 (market); Alistair Michael Thomas/Shutterstock, pg. 86 (Lumpini
Park); guruXOX/Shutterstock, pg. 89 (skiers); Ocean Image Photography/
Shutterstock, pg. 89 (surfer); ClassicStock/Alamy, pg. 95 (Wright brothers);
Monkey Business Images/Shutterstock, pg. 95 (woman in office); mamezito/
Shutterstock, pg. 95 (dollar bills); ClassicStock/Alamy, pg. 97 (Wright
brothers); Keystone-France/Contributor/Getty Images, pg. 97 (old-fashioned
camera); Alex Segre/Alamy, pg. 97 (phone camera); Hilary Morgan/Alamy,
pg. 100 (steamship); Corbis, pg. 100 (Wright brothers plane); GraphicaArtis/
Contributor/Getty Images, pg. 103 (Boulevard Du Temple, Paris); Ron
Chapple/Corbis, pg. 109 (truck driver); InStock/Image Source/Corbis, pg.
109 (worker and employer); Florian Küttler/Westend61/Corbis, pg. 109
(pharmacist); Christopher Futcher/Getty Images, pg. 109 (doctor); Monkey
Business Images/Shutterstock, pg. 109 (woman in office); Mascarucci/Corbis,
pg. 109 (waiter).

REVIEWERS

We would like to acknowledge the following individuals for their input during the development of the series:

Mahmoud Al-Salah
University of Dammam
Saudi Arabia

Robert J. Ashcroft
Tokai University
Japan

Karen E. Caldwell
Bahrain Polytechnic
Bahrain

Stephanie da Costa Mello
Glendale Community College
U.S.A.

Travis Cote
Tamagawa University
Japan

Ian Daniels
Smart ELT
Japan

Gail Fernandez
Bergen Community College
U.S.A.

Theresa Garcia de Quevedo
Geos Boston English Language School
U.S.A.

Patricia Ishill
Union County College
U.S.A.

Ji Hoon Kim
Independence English Institute
South Korea

Masakazu Kimura
Katoh Gakuen Gyoshu High School/
Nihon University
Japan

Georgios-Vlasios Kormpas
Al Yamamah University/SILC
Saudi Arabia

Ji-seon Lee
Jeong English Campus
South Korea

Sang-lee Lee
Kangleong Community Language
Center
South Korea

Zee Eun Lim
Reader's Mate
South Korea

James MacDonald
Aspire Language Academy
Kaohsiung City

Chaker Ali Mhamdi
Al Buraimi University College
Oman

Elizabeth R. Neblett
Union County College
U.S.A.

John Peloghitis
Tokai University
Japan

Whitney Tullos
Intrax
U.S.A.

Pingtang Yen
Eden Institute
Taichung City

Author Acknowledgments

A special thanks to my mentor in Teaching English as a Second Language at Northeastern Illinois University, Dr. Teddy Bofman, who counseled me that education is never over. A thank you to my students at the Illinois Institute of Technology for sharing their opinions, thoughts, and pursuits with me and to the community of faculty and friends I've met along the way.

Many thanks to Eliza Jensen for her discerning eye and diligent work on *Trio Reading* and to Anna Norris for sharing her enthusiasm and opinions in developing this series. Both were valuable collaborators.

And a thank you to my husband and son, my lifelong learning partners.

—Kate Adams

CONTENTS

UNIT 2 Places *(continued)*

5 **How Does the World Communicate?** page 70	**Reading 1:** Why Is English a Global Language? **Reading 2:** Why Do Languages Die?	Oxford 2000 🔑 words to talk about communication Short u /ʌ/ sound ◑ **Make connections:** Text to self	Use a dictionary Summarize Count and noncount nouns; *a/an* + singular count nouns ◑ **Make connections:** Text to text	Summarizing and retelling ◑ **Make connections:** Text to world
6 **Why Do We Go on Vacation?** page 82	**Reading 1:** Finding Excitement and Calm in the City **Reading 2:** Do Vacations Bring Happiness?	Oxford 2000 🔑 words to talk about vacation Long o /oʊ/ and short i /ɪ/ sounds ◑ **Make connections:** Text to self	Comparative and superlative adjectives Visualize *does not* and *do not* + verbs; *always, often, never* with verbs ◑ **Make connections:** Text to text	Summarizing and retelling ◑ **Make connections:** Text to world

> **UNIT WRAP UP** Extend Your Skills page 94

UNIT 3 Things pages 95–132

CHAPTER	READINGS	▲ BEFORE READING	▲▲ DURING READING	▲▲▲ AFTER READING
7 **What Inventions Changed the World?** page 96	**Reading 1:** The Way We Travel **Reading 2:** It's in a Picture	Oxford 2000 🔑 words to talk about inventions Long i /ɑɪ/ sound ◑ **Make connections:** Text to self	Word families Signal words for time Simple past; *was* and *were* ◑ **Make connections:** Text to text	Summarizing and retelling ◑ **Make connections:** Text to world
8 **Jobs and Skills in the 21st Century** page 108	**Reading 1:** What Jobs Are We Going to Need? **Reading 2:** What Skills Do Businesses Want?	Oxford 2000 🔑 words to talk about jobs Schwa /ə/ and long e /i/ ◑ **Make connections:** Text to self	Suffix *-er* Identify pronoun references *the* + nouns; verbs + *about* ◑ **Make connections:** Text to text	Summarizing and retelling ◑ **Make connections:** Text to world
9 **Money Matters** page 120	**Reading 1:** Banks, Then and Now **Reading 2:** How to Set a Budget	Oxford 2000 🔑 words to talk about money Long a /eɪ/ sound ◑ **Make connections:** Text to self	Financial collocations Analyze charts and spreadsheets *want to* + verbs; present progressive ◑ **Make connections:** Text to text	Summarizing and retelling ◑ **Make connections:** Text to world

> **UNIT WRAP UP** Extend Your Skills page 132

The Oxford 2000 🔑 List of Keywords pages 133–142

Welcome to Trio Reading

Building Better Readers . . . From the Beginning

Trio Reading includes three levels of Student Books, Online Practice, and Teacher Support.

Level 1/CEFR A1   Level 2/CEFR A2   Level 3/CEFR B1

Essential Digital Content   iTools USB with Classroom Resources

   Trio Reading's contextualized vocabulary instruction, accessible paired readings, and critical thinking activities provide students with the tools they need for successful academic reading at the earliest stages of language acquisition.

Vocabulary Based On the Oxford 2000 🔑 Keywords

   Trio Reading's vocabulary is based on the 2,000 most important and useful words to learn at the early stages of language learning, making content approachable for low-level learners.

Making Connections for Critical Thinking

   Make Connections sections encourage the development of critical thinking skills by asking learners to draw connections between themselves, texts, and the world around them.

Readiness Unit

   For added flexibility, each level of *Trio Reading* begins with an optional Readiness Unit to provide fundamental English tools for beginning students.

INSIDE EACH CHAPTER

▲ BEFORE READING

Theme-based chapters set a context for learning.

Essential, explicit skills help beginning learners to gain confidence with academic reading texts.

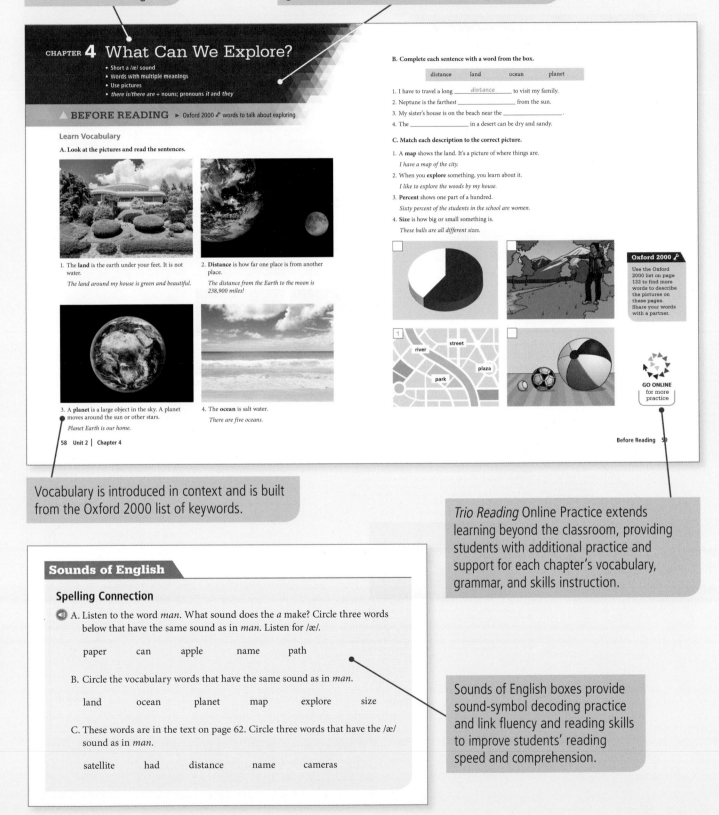

CHAPTER **4** What Can We Explore?

- Short a /æ/ sound
- Words with multiple meanings
- Use pictures
- *there is/there are* + nouns; pronouns *it* and *they*

▲ **BEFORE READING** ▶ Oxford 2000 🔑 words to talk about exploring

Learn Vocabulary

A. Look at the pictures and read the sentences.

1. The **land** is the earth under your feet. It is not water.
   The land around my house is green and beautiful.

2. **Distance** is how far one place is from another place.
   The distance from the Earth to the moon is 238,900 miles!

3. A **planet** is a large object in the sky. A planet moves around the sun or other stars.
   Planet Earth is our home.

4. The **ocean** is salt water.
   There are five oceans.

58   Unit 2 | Chapter 4

B. Complete each sentence with a word from the box.

distance	land	ocean	planet

1. I have to travel a long ___*distance*___ to visit my family.
2. Neptune is the farthest _____ from the sun.
3. My sister's house is on the beach near the _____ .
4. The _____ in a desert can be dry and sandy.

C. Match each description to the correct picture.

1. A **map** shows the land. It's a picture of where things are.
   I have a map of the city.
2. When you **explore** something, you learn about it.
   I like to explore the woods by my house.
3. **Percent** shows one part of a hundred.
   Sixty percent of the students in the school are women.
4. **Size** is how big or small something is.
   These balls are all different sizes.

Oxford 2000 🔑
Use the Oxford 2000 list on page 133 to find more words to describe the pictures on these pages. Share your words with a partner.

GO ONLINE
for more
practice

Before Reading   59

Vocabulary is introduced in context and is built from the Oxford 2000 list of keywords.

Trio Reading Online Practice extends learning beyond the classroom, providing students with additional practice and support for each chapter's vocabulary, grammar, and skills instruction.

Sounds of English

Spelling Connection

🔊 A. Listen to the word *man*. What sound does the *a* make? Circle three words below that have the same sound as in *man*. Listen for /æ/.

paper	can	apple	name	path

B. Circle the vocabulary words that have the same sound as in *man*.

land	ocean	planet	map	explore	size

C. These words are in the text on page 62. Circle three words that have the /æ/ sound as in *man*.

satellite	had	distance	name	cameras

Sounds of English boxes provide sound-symbol decoding practice and link fluency and reading skills to improve students' reading speed and comprehension.

DURING READING

Accessible paired readings help students develop reading skills by offering more reading practice and the opportunity to make connections between texts.

Vocabulary Strategies and Reading Strategies are practiced with each reading, giving students the skills they need for successful reading.

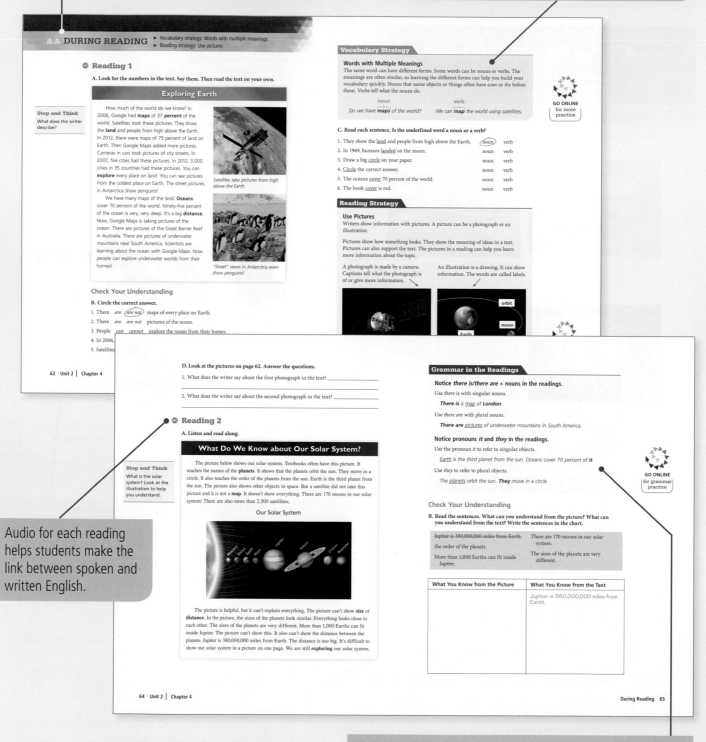

DURING READING ▶ Vocabulary strategy: Words with multiple meanings
▶ Reading strategy: Use pictures

Reading 1

A. Look for the numbers in the text. Say them. Then read the text on your own.

Exploring Earth

Stop and Think
What does the writer describe?

How much of the world do we know? In 2006, Google had **maps** of 37 **percent** of the world. Satellites took these pictures. They show the **land** and people from high above the Earth. In 2012, there were maps of 75 percent of land on Earth. Then Google Maps added more pictures. Cameras in cars took pictures of city streets. In 2007, five cities had these pictures. In 2012, 3,000 cities in 35 countries had these pictures. You can **explore** every place on land. You can see pictures from the coldest place on Earth. The street pictures in Antarctica show penguins!

We have many maps of the land. **Oceans** cover 70 percent of the world. Ninety-five percent of the ocean is very, very deep. It's a big **distance**. Now, Google Maps is taking pictures of the ocean. There are pictures of the Great Barrier Reef in Australia. There are pictures of underwater mountains near South America. Scientists are learning about the ocean with Google Maps. Now people can explore underwater worlds from their homes!

Satellites take pictures from high above the Earth.

"Street" views in Antarctica even show penguins!

Check Your Understanding

B. Circle the correct answer.

1. There *are* (*are not*) maps of every place on Earth.
2. There *are* *are not* pictures of the ocean.
3. People *can* *cannot* explore the ocean from their homes.
4. In 2006,
5. Satellites

Vocabulary Strategy

Words with Multiple Meanings
The same word can have different forms. Some words can be nouns or verbs. The meanings are often similar, so learning the different forms can help you build your vocabulary quickly. Nouns that name objects or things often have *a/an* or *the* before them. Verbs tell what the nouns do.

noun	verb
Do we have **maps** *of the world?*	*We can* **map** *the world using satellites.*

C. Read each sentence. Is the underlined word a noun or a verb?

1. They show the <u>land</u> and people from high above the Earth. (noun) verb
2. In 1969, humans <u>landed</u> on the moon. noun verb
3. Draw a big <u>circle</u> on your paper. noun verb
4. <u>Circle</u> the correct answer. noun verb
5. The oceans <u>cover</u> 70 percent of the world. noun verb
6. The book <u>cover</u> is red. noun verb

Reading Strategy

Use Pictures
Writers show information with pictures. A picture can be a photograph or an illustration.

Pictures show how something looks. They show the meaning of ideas in a text. Pictures can also support the text. The pictures in a reading can help you learn more information about the topic.

A photograph is made by a camera. Captions tell what the photograph is of or give more information.

An illustration is a drawing. It can show information. The words are called labels.

GO ONLINE for more practice

D. Look at the pictures on page 62. Answer the questions.

1. What does the writer say about the first photograph in the text? _____

2. What does the writer say about the second photograph in the text? _____

Reading 2

A. Listen and read along.

What Do We Know about Our Solar System?

Stop and Think
What is the solar system? Look at the illustration to help you understand.

The picture below shows our solar system. Textbooks often have this picture. It teaches the names of the **planets**. It shows that the planets orbit the sun. They move in a circle. It also teaches the order of the planets from the sun. Earth is the third planet from the sun. The picture also shows other objects in space. But a satellite did not take this picture and it is not a **map**. It doesn't show everything. There are 170 moons in our solar system! There are also more than 2,500 satellites.

Our Solar System

The picture is helpful, but it can't explain everything. The picture can't show **size** or **distance**. In the picture, the sizes of the planets look similar. Everything looks close to each other. The sizes of the planets are very different. More than 1,000 Earths can fit inside Jupiter. The picture can't show this. It also can't show the distance between the planets. Jupiter is 380,000,000 miles from Earth. The distance is too big. It's difficult to show our solar system in a picture on one page. We are still **exploring** our solar system.

Grammar in the Readings

Notice *there is/there are* + nouns in the readings.
Use *there is* with singular nouns.
There is *a* <u>map</u> *of* **London.**
Use *there are* with plural nouns.
There are <u>pictures</u> *of underwater mountains in South America.*

Notice pronouns *it* and *they* in the readings.
Use the pronoun *it* to refer to singular objects.
<u>Earth</u> *is the third planet from the sun. Oceans cover 70 percent of* **it.**
Use *they* to refer to plural objects.
The <u>planets</u> *orbit the sun.* **They** *move in a circle.*

GO ONLINE for grammar practice

Check Your Understanding

B. Read the sentences. What can you understand from the picture? What can you understand from the text? Write the sentences in the chart.

Jupiter is 380,000,000 miles from Earth.
the order of the planets
More than 1,000 Earths can fit inside Jupiter.

There are 170 moons in our solar system.
The sizes of the planets are very different.

What You Know from the Picture	What You Know from the Text
	Jupiter is 380,000,000 miles from Earth.

Audio for each reading helps students make the link between spoken and written English.

Grammar in the Readings boxes highlight the most important language from the readings. Practice of each grammar point is provided as part of *Trio Reading* Online Practice.

▲▲▲ AFTER READING

Summarizing and Retelling activities provide students with the opportunity to review the concepts and vocabulary learned throughout the chapter.

Three Make Connections sections in each chapter help students develop critical thinking skills by linking texts to their own lives, other texts, and the wider world.

▲▲▲ AFTER READING

Summarizing and Retelling

A. Complete the sentences with the words from the box. Some of the words have to be changed to fit the sentences. For example, *map* has to be changed to *maps*. Then read the paragraphs to a partner to summarize.

Nouns	Verbs
distance	explore
land	
map	
ocean	
percent	
planet	
size	

1. In the first text, the topic is _____. The writer says that we can use Google Maps to _____ the world. We have pictures from satellites in the sky. They show the _____. He says that there are maps of the land and _____. The ocean covers 70 _____ of Earth, but it's deep and difficult to explore.

2. In the second text, the writer talks about the _____. He tells the order they are in from the sun. He tells that pictures don't always show the truth. The solar system is so big. It's hard to show the _____ between the planets in an illustration. And it's difficult to show the _____ of the planets.

B. Both writers use pronouns. Find each sentence in the text on page 62 or 64. Circle the word the pronoun refers to.

1. **They** show the land and people from high above the Earth.
   a. pictures   b. planets
2. But a satellite did not take this picture and **it** is not a map.
   a. space   b. picture
3. **It** teaches the names of the planets.
   a. picture   b. solar system
4. **It** also can't show the distance between the planets.
   a. Jupiter   b. picture
5. **They** move in a circle.
   a. planets   b. sun

Word Partners

reach land

live off the land

develop the land

own land

piece of land

GO ONLINE
to practice
word partners ▶◀

● Make Connections: Text to World

A. Think about texts that explain. Check the statements you agree with.

1. _____ Pictures are helpful, but they can't explain some things.
2. _____ We can learn about our world from photos.
3. _____ Texts are better than pictures and maps at sharing ideas.
4. _____ Pictures can show things that the text cannot.
5. _____ Good writers use pictures or maps to show information.

B. Write ideas that you like to read about in each type of text. Then answer the questions below.

Texts That Explain

Newspapers	Magazines	Textbooks
_____	_____	_____
_____	_____	_____
_____	_____	_____

1. What pictures, maps, or illustrations do you see in these texts?
_____

2. When do writers use numbers in these texts?
_____

3. What words or phrases do writers use when they explain ideas?
_____

4. What information do captions and labels give?
_____

C. Talk about your answers from Activities A and B with a partner. Look at the Oxford 2000 keywords on page 133 and find five words to help you.

Chant

GO ONLINE
for the
Chapter 4
Vocabulary &
Grammar Chant

Word Partners activities expand on vocabulary taught in the chapter so students acquire more high-frequency collocations.

Vocabulary and Grammar Chants found online help students internalize the target grammar structure and vocabulary for greater fluency when reading.

Trio Reading Online Practice: Essential Digital Content

Trio Reading Online Practice provides multiple opportunities for skills practice and acquisition—beyond the classroom and beyond the page.

Each unit of *Trio Reading* is accompanied by a variety of automatically graded activities. Students' progress is recorded, tracked, and fed back to the instructor.

Vocabulary and Grammar Chants help students internalize the target grammar structure and vocabulary for greater accuracy and fluency when reading.

Grammar Note *I am (not)* + adjectives
Put the words in the correct order to make a sentence.

1. [I] [am] [friendly] [.]

2. [I] [am] [not] [sad] [.]

3. [.] [happy] [am] [I]

4. [Nice] [am] [.] [I]

5. [Am] [I] [mad] [not] [.]

6. [.] [am] [not] [short] [I]

Reset

Submit

Online Activities provide essential practice of Vocabulary, Grammar, and Reading and Vocabulary Strategies.

Grammar in the Readings

Notice *there is/there are* + nouns in the readings.
Use *there is* with singular nouns.
   There is a *map* of **London**.
Use *there are* with plural nouns.
   There are *pictures* of underwater mountains in South America.

Notice pronouns *it* and *they* in the readings.
Use the pronoun *it* to refer to singular objects.
   Earth is the third planet from the sun. Oceans cover 70 percent of *it*.
Use *they* to refer to plural objects.
   The *planets* orbit the sun. **They** move in a circle.

GO ONLINE for grammar practice

Vocabulary and Grammar Chants provide further accuracy and fluency practice for every chapter.

exciting

What characteristics make something an adventure?

Chant
GO ONLINE for the Chapter 6 Vocabulary & Grammar Chant

GO ONLINE icons lead students to essential digital content.

Use the access code on the inside front cover to log in at **www.oxfordlearn.com/login**.

Readiness Unit

Words

The alphabet
Letters and sounds
Syllables

Parts of Speech

Nouns
Adjectives
Verbs

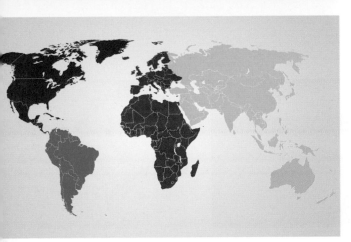

Sentences and Paragraphs

Sentences
Paragraphs
Make connections

UNIT WRAP UP Extend Your Skills

The alphabet

The English alphabet has 26 letters:

a b c d e f g h i j k l m n o p q r s t u v w x y z

A. Write the missing letters from the English alphabet.

1. ab _c_ de __ ghij __ lmnopq __ stu __ wx __ z

2. a __ cd __ fg __ ijkl __ nop __ rstuv __ xyz

B. Write the letters in the correct order of the alphabet.

1. m d w g b o a q   _a b d g m o q w_

2. z u w l t e h j   _____

3. i k p c f y r s   _____

4. p e s y g m r I   _____

Letters make words.

man

pen

book

C. Write the missing letters.

1. g _i_ rl

2. __ up

3. __ a __ y

D. Circle the words that have the letter _r_.

read   you   write   look   chair

> When a word **begins** with a letter, that letter is first. These words begin with the letter _s_.
>
>   _s_ay   _s_ee   _s_aw   _s_ome   _s_ick

E. Circle the words that begin with the letter _w_.

write   world   meet   saw   work

F. Circle the words that begin with the letter _b_.

be   pen   bite   dad   boat

> When a word **ends** with a letter, that letter is last. These words end with the letter _e_.
>
>   writ_e_   m_e_   w_e_   giv_e_   mak_e_

G. Circle the words that end with the letter _d_.

understand   read   do   world   rub

H. Circle the words that end with the letter _m_.

man   mom   law   come   from

> When a letter or letters are in the **middle** of a word, the letter or letters come between the beginning and ending letters. These letters are in the middle.
>
>   d_i_g   a_ct_   m_ea_n   c_om_e   g_e_t

I. Circle the words that have the letter _a_ in the middle.

dad   but   parent   grand   apple

J. Circle the words that have the letter _k_ in the middle.

take   kick   make   hot   break

K. Write the missing letter from each word. If you need help, look at the words on this page.

1. a _c_ t   2. ___ ig   3. f ___ om

4. ma ___ e   5. pa ___ ent

Letters and sounds

Say the name of the letters of the alphabet:

a b c d e f g h i j k l m n o p q r s t u v w x y z

These letters are vowels:

a e i o u

Sometimes they make the sound of their letter name. Other times they make a different sound.

> When does a vowel say its letter name?
>
> When there are two vowels or a vowel with *y*, say the name of the first vowel.
>
> > *dream   sea   coach   say*
>
> When there is a vowel-consonant-*e*, say the name of the first vowel. The *e* at the end does not have a sound.
>
> > *cake   kite   vote   cute   these*

Sometimes the vowels make a short sound. Look at the symbol. Read the word. Listen to the sound.

a /æ/	*at*		o /ɑ/	*hot*	
e /ɛ/	*ten*		u /ʌ/	*cup*	
i /ɪ/	*sit*				

The other letters are consonants:

b c d f g h j k l m n p q r s t v w x y z

Say the sound of the consonants at the beginning of each word. Listen to the sounds.

p	*pen*	s	*so*
b	*bad*	z	*zoo*
t	*tea*	sh	*she*
d	*did*	h	*how*
c / k	*cat / kick*	m	*man*
g	*got*	n	*no*
ch	*chin*	l	*leg*
j	*June*	r	*red*
f	*fall*	y	*yes*
v	*voice*	w	*wet*
th	*thin*		

When you read a word, you say the sounds of the letters.

man /mæn/   pen /pɛn/   book /bʊk/

A. These words begin with the same sound. Say the words and listen for the /b/ sound.

book   ball   be   bank

B. Say the words. Cross out the word that does not have the same beginning sound.

1. man   make   ~~name~~   my

2. like   ice   lot   listen

3. add   odd   at   active

C. These words end with the same sound. Say the words and listen for the /t/ sound.

get   text   wet   late

D. Say the words. Cross out the word that does not have the same ending sound.

1. read   understand   ~~that~~   made

2. come   mean   from   exclaim

3. think   frog   kick   cake

E. These words have the same vowel sound in the middle. Say the words and listen for the /ɪ/ sound.

lip   fit   bit

F. Say the words. Cross out the word that does not have the same vowel sound.

1. cat   map   sat   ~~make~~

2. male   take   seat   wait

3. tell   bed   get   sea

G. Say the words. Listen to how many sounds are in each word.

cat ⟶ /kæt/   make ⟶ /meɪk/   book ⟶ /bʊk/

3 sounds   **3 sounds**   **3 sounds**

H. Say the words. Circle the number of sounds.

1. want   2   3   ④

2. bake   2   3   4

3. do   2   3   4

4. goal   2   3   4

These words rhyme. Only the beginning sound is different.

make   take   fake

I. Cross out the word that does not rhyme.

1. egg   leg   ~~flag~~   peg

2. pack   black   crack   fact

3. meet   feet   sea   meat

J. Match each word to a word that rhymes.

1. __b__ white   a. lay

2. _____ fat   b. bite

3. _____ bit   c. die

4. _____ lie   d. mat

5. _____ may   e. fit

Syllables

Words are made of syllables. Each syllable has a vowel sound. Say each syllable in the words below.

text	your•self	un•der•stand
1	1 2	1 2 3

The letter *y* can sound like a vowel.

It sounds like a long i /aɪ/ in a one-syllable word.

    fly   my   cry

It sounds like a long e /i/ when a consonant is before it and it ends a two-syllable word.

    ba•by

A. Write the number of syllables in the words below.

1. lady   by   many   lie

   2   _____   _____   _____

2. read   text   make   to

_____   _____   _____   _____

3. self   myself   home   flat

_____   _____   _____   _____

B. Cross out the word that has a different number of syllables.

1. write   now   say   ~~city~~
2. funny   detail   world   empty
3. ice   nice   finish   do
4. think   tell   go   notice
5. person   man   discuss   woman

Nouns

Some words are nouns. These words name people, places, and things.

People	Places	Things
boy	*park*	*cup*
girl	*school*	*map*
woman	*home*	*sun*

A. Look at each picture. Write the noun.

1. _____

2. _____

3. _____

When there is one of a noun, it is singular. When there is more than one, it is plural.
Add -s to the noun.

B. Is there one or more than one in each picture? Write the correct noun.

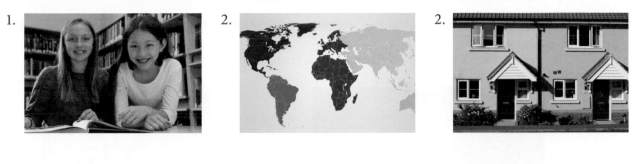

1. _____

2. _____

2. _____

Adjectives

Some words are adjectives. They tell about nouns.

Numbers	Colors	Other Descriptions
one girl	*red* shirt	**Adjectives tell about size.** *small* box
two boys	*blue* pants	*big* box **Adjectives tell about feelings.**
three men	*green* socks	*sad* boy
four women	*black* hair	*happy* girl

A. Circle the adjective in each phrase.

1. the (tall) building

2. the blue water

3. the small baby

4. the sad boy

5. the beautiful sky

6. the white moon

B. Look at each picture. Write a phrase from Activity A.

1.

the white moon

2.

3.

4.

5.

6.

You can write numbers as words.

1 one   2 two   3 three   4 four   5 five   6 six   7 seven   8 eight   9 nine   10 ten

C. Look at each picture. Write the number and the noun.

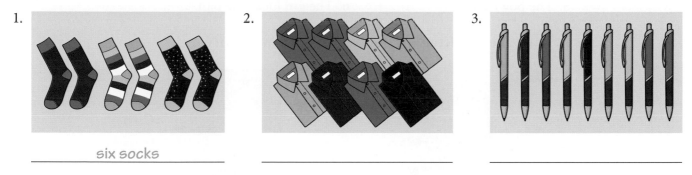

1. _____ six socks _____

2. _____

3. _____

Verbs

Some words are verbs. Some verbs show action. They tell what nouns do. Other verbs tell what nouns are. We call these verbs *linking verbs* because they link a noun to another noun or adjective.

	Action Verbs (Tell What Nouns Do)	Linking Verbs (Tell What Nouns Are)
	The girls <u>jump</u>.	*The girls <u>are</u> young.*
	The man <u>reads</u>.	*The man <u>is</u> busy.*
	The snow <u>falls</u>.	*The snow <u>is</u> cold.*
	The boy <u>raises</u> his hand.	*The boy <u>is</u> a student.*

A. Circle the verb in each sentence.

1. The woman (is) a teacher.   2. The man listens.

3. The sun rises.   4. The desks are white.

5. The boy runs.   6. The girl kicks the ball.

B. Look at each picture. Write a sentence from Activity A.

1.

The man listens.

2.

_____

3.

_____

4.

_____

5.

_____

6.

_____

C. Which words are nouns, which are adjectives, and which are verbs? Write them in the chart.

woman reads

big world

little circle

sad girl

small letters

man writes

Adjectives	Nouns	Verbs
big		

Sentences

A sentence tells an idea. Use words to write sentences. The words have spaces between them.

I like to read.
1 2 3 4

A sentence begins with a capital letter and ends with a period.

capital letter   period
We enjoy reading.

Look at the capital letters of the alphabet.

A B C D E F G H I J K L M N O P Q R S T U V W X Y Z

A. Circle the number of words in each sentence.

1. Words are made of letters.	3	4	(5)	6
2. Sentences are made of words.	3	4	5	6
3. I read books.	3	4	5	6
4. My mom gave me a book.	3	4	5	6

A sentence can ask a question. A question ends with a question mark and needs an answer. Some questions have *yes* or *no* answers.

question mark

Question: *Do you like to read?*   Answer: *Yes, I like to read.*

Some questions ask for information.

Question: *What time is it?*   Answer: *It is 9 o'clock.*

Read the questions and the answers.

	Information Questions	Answers
Things	**What** food do you like?	I like apples.
Places	**Where** are you from?	I am from India.
Time	**When** do you eat dinner?	I eat dinner at 7 o'clock.
Type	**What kind** of books do you like?	I like books about history.
People	**Who** do you eat with?	I eat with my friends.
Reason	**Why** do you study English?	I study English for my job.

Every sentence has a verb. In English, the noun comes before the verb.

noun   verb
The woman drives.

Sometimes the verb is followed by another noun.

noun   verb   noun
The woman drives the car.

Sometimes the verb is followed by an adjective.

verb   adjective
I am tired.

B. Put each group of words in order to make a sentence. Use a capital letter and period.

1. home / walks / the boy   The boy walks home. _____

2. the test / the students / take   _____

3. the book / I / understand   _____

4. funny / is / he   _____

The noun does not come before the verb in questions. The question word comes first.

How are you?	*Who is that?*	*When is the meeting?*
Where are you going?	*Why are you mad?*	*What is your name?*

C. Put each group of words in order to make a question. Use a capital letter and question mark.

1. you / who / are   Who are you? _____

2. is / the class / when   _____

3. why / you / are / sad   _____

4. are / you / where   _____

D. Match each question with its answer.

1. What do you like? __b__

2. Where are you from? _____

3. Do you study English? _____

4. Why are you sad? _____

5. Are you OK? _____

a. No, I study French.

b. I like to read.

c. I am sick.

d. Yes, I am fine.

e. I am from Jordan.

Paragraphs

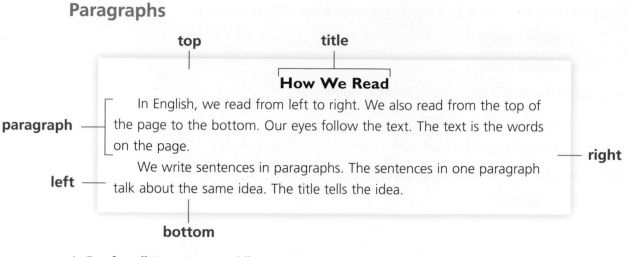

A. Look at "How We Read." Complete each sentence with a word from the box.

read	right	text	top	~~two~~

1. There are _____ two _____ paragraphs.

2. The title is "How We _____."

3. We read from left to _____.

4. We also read from _____ to bottom.

5. The _____ is the words on the page.

B. Read the paragraph. Answer the questions.

> ### Beautiful by the Sea
> I am from Turkey. I live by the sea. I love it there. It is beautiful. I love my home.

1. Circle the number of sentences.   3   4   5

2. Write the title. _____

3. Circle the number of paragraphs.   1   3   5

C. Read each paragraph. Answer the questions.

> In the English language, we read from left to right. This is the order of the words. We also read from the top of the page to the bottom. Our eyes follow the text.

1. How many sentences are in the paragraph?   3   4   5

2. Write three verbs from the paragraph.

_____ _____ _____

3. How many times do you see *read* in the paragraph?   2   3   4

> In English, every sentence has a verb. Most sentences also have nouns. Verbs tell what nouns do. We write sentences with nouns and verbs.

4. How many sentences are in the paragraph?   2   3   4

5. Write three nouns from the paragraph.

_____   _____   _____

6. How many times do you see *sentence* in the paragraph?   2   3   4

7. What is a good title for the paragraph?   *Sentences*   *Verbs*

◐ Make Connections

Text to Self

A. Circle the best answer.

1. Do you read from left to right in your language?	Yes	No
2. Do sentences in your language need verbs?	Yes	No
3. Does your language use letters?	Yes	No

Text to Text

B. Look at the two texts in Paragraphs Activity C. How are they the same? How are they different? Complete each sentence with a word from the box.

sentences	English	order

1. The two texts talk about _____.

2. The first paragraph talks about the _____ of the words. We read from left to right.

3. The second paragraph talks about words in _____. Every sentence needs a verb.

Text to World

C. Answer the questions with a partner. Look at the Oxford 2000 keywords on page 133 and find words to help you.

1. What do you like to read?

2. Why do people read?

3. Why do texts have titles?

Look at the word bank for the Readiness Unit. Check (✓) the words you know.
Circle the words you want to learn better.

OXFORD 2000 🔑

Adjectives		Nouns				Verbs
beautiful	one	alphabet	hair	right	water	be (is/are)
big	red	baby	hand	school	woman	fall
black	sad	ball	home	sentence	world	follow
blue	seven	book	left	shirt		have
busy	six	bottom	letter	sky		jump
cold	small	box	man	snow		kick
eight	tall	boy	map	sock		listen
five	ten	building	moon	student		raise
four	three	circle	order	sun		read
green	two	cup	pants	teacher		run
happy	white	desk	paragraph	text		tell
little	young	English	park	title		use
nine		girl	pen	top		write

PRACTICE WITH THE OXFORD 2000 🔑

A. Use the words in the chart. Match adjectives with nouns.

1. _____big school_____   2. _____

3. _____   4. _____

5. _____

B. Use the words in the chart. Match verbs with nouns.

1. _____use a map_____   2. _____

3. _____   4. _____

5. _____

C. Use the words in the chart. Match verbs with adjective noun partners.

1. _____have one pen_____   2. _____

3. _____   4. _____

5. _____

UNIT **1** People

UNIT WRAP UP Extend Your Skills

CHAPTER 1

How Are Family Members Alike?

- Short e /ɛ/ sound
- Collocations with *get*
- Find the topic
- *we* + verbs *they* + verbs

▲ BEFORE READING ► Oxford 2000 ✎ words to talk about family

Learn Vocabulary

A. Match each picture to the correct sentence.

_____ A **characteristic** is something you are or have, like the color of your eyes.

_____ A **member** is a person who is in a group, like a sports team.

___1___ A **family** is a group of people, like parents and children.

_____ When you **notice** something, you see it.

1.

2.

3.

Eyes: Brown

4.

B. Match each picture to the correct sentence.

_____ The **height** of something or someone is the distance from the top to the bottom.

_____ If you are **short**, you are not as tall as other people.

___1__ If you are **tall**, you grow higher than other people.

_____ When children grow, they **get** taller.

1.

2.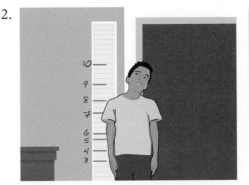

3.

4.

C. Complete each sentence with a word from the box.

Oxford 2000 🔑

Use the Oxford 2000 list on page 133 to find more words to describe the pictures on these pages. Share your words with a partner.

| characteristics | get | ~~members~~ | short |
| family | height | notice | tall |

1. My family _____members_____ have brown hair.

2. My _____ has dinner together on Saturdays.

3. My children _____ taller every year.

4. People _____ me because I have red hair.

5. Most basketball players are _____.

6. My sister is _____, but my brother is tall.

7. We have two _____ that are the same: our height and our eyes.

8. She is very tall. People notice her because of her _____.

GO ONLINE for more practice

Preview the Text

D. Look at the picture on page 24. Answer the questions.

1. What is in the picture? _____

2. What is the relationship of the people in the photo? _____

3. What characteristics do the people share? _____

E. Look at the text on page 24. Answer the questions.

1. What is the title? _____

2. What do you think the writer talks about in the text?

_____

3. The text _____ .

    a. explains something   b. describes someone

Sounds of English

Spelling Connection

A. Listen to the word *text*. What sound does the *e* make? Circle four words below that have the same sound as in *text*. Listen for /ɛ/.

    met   bed   late   tea   rest   pet

B. Circle the vocabulary words that have the short e sound as in *text*.

    family   get   height   characteristic

    member   notice   short   tall

C. These words are in the text on page 24. Circle two words that have the short e /ɛ/ sound as in *text*.

    red   we   legs   sister

● ● Make Connections: Text to Self

A. Answer the questions. Use words from the box to help you.

characteristics	get	members	short
family	height	notice	tall

1. What can you learn from a family picture? _____

_____

2. Why do people take family pictures? _____

_____

3. Write two characteristics that your family has. _____

_____

B. Think about your family. Complete the chart.

How many family
members are there?

_____

_____

What do people notice
about you?

_____

_____

How are you like your family?

_____

Who do you look like?

_____

_____

What is different about you?

_____

_____

C. Think about why people write about themselves and their families. Answer the questions.

1. Why do people write about themselves? _____

_____

2. Why do people read about others? _____

_____

3. What do you like to learn about other people? _____

_____

▲▲ DURING READING
▶ Vocabulary strategy: Collocations with *get*
▶ Reading strategy: Find the topic

◉ Reading 1

A. First listen to the text. There is a short pause at a period. Mark the pauses you hear.

I have a big family.|There are six people in my family.

↖

B. Now read the text on your own. Pause at the end of each sentence.

Stop and Think

Read the title. Look at the picture. How is the writer like her family?

How Am I Like My Family?

   I have a big **family**. There are six people in my family. I have one sister and two brothers. We are all very **tall**. We get our height from my parents. My father and mother are both tall. Our **height** is one **characteristic** that we all have. Our height helps us in sports. My brothers and sister and I play soccer. We have long legs. We can run fast. We really like to run. We are good at soccer. We get better every year. We love to play!

   I have one characteristic that is different from my family. When we **get** together, people **notice** me. My hair color is different. My family **members** have brown hair. My hair is red! I don't know why. Maybe it is from my grandfather. He has red hair, too. All the members of my family are tall, but only I have red hair.

Check Your Understanding

C. Circle the correct answer.

1. The writer is   (tall)   short.

2. The writer has   *brown   red*   hair.

3. The brothers and sisters like   *soccer   basketball*.

4. The writer has red hair. Her   *mother   grandfather*   also has red hair.

5. People   *notice   don't notice*   the writer.

24   Unit 1 | Chapter 1

Vocabulary Strategy

Collocations with *get*

Collocations are words that go together. Learning collocations helps you build your vocabulary. The verb *get* is used in many collocations.

When you *get* something, you receive it.   *Get* can also mean *become*.

   *A good athlete **gets** a lot of attention.*   *Children **get** taller.*

Notice the collocations with the verb *get* in the readings.

GO ONLINE
for more practice

D. Read the text on page 24 again. Check the words the writer uses after the verb *get*.

1. _✓_ our height   2. _____ better

3. _____ soccer   4. _____ run

5. _____ family   6. _____ together

E. Complete each sentence with a phrase from the box.

| ~~get along~~ | get excited | get scared | get home |

1. I like my brothers. We _____ get along _____ well.

2. My parents _____ at 6:00 p.m. every day.

3. My sisters and I _____ up high. We don't like heights.

4. I _____ about traveling. I love to visit new places.

Reading Strategy

Find the Topic

Finding the topic of a reading can help you understand the text. Use these strategies to help you find the topic.

1. Look at the title. Read the first and last sentences.
2. Look for repeated words (words used again and again).
3. Look at the other words. What do they tell about?

GO ONLINE
for more practice

F. Write a short answer to each question.

1. What word is in both the title and the first sentence? _____

2. Write words that are repeated in the first paragraph. _____

3. Write words that are repeated in the second paragraph. _____

4. Look at the words used in the text. What do the words tell about? _____

5. What is the topic of the reading? _____

◉ Reading 2

A. **Listen to the text. Mark the pauses you hear.**

B. **Read the text on your own. Pause at the end of each sentence.**

Who Is Lionel Messi?

Many people think Lionel Messi is the best soccer player in the world. He is the youngest person to score a goal in the international league. He was 16 years old! How did he do it? Did he have a great teacher? Is it from his **family**? Lionel has two older brothers and a younger sister. When he was a boy, he played soccer with his older brothers. He was not scared to play with older kids. He didn't have a teacher. He loved to play. He was very good. Coaches noticed his skill. They wanted him on their team. Lionel is the only family **member** who plays soccer in the international league. It is his job. The other kids liked to play soccer, but Lionel's skill is special.

Lionel Messi

Lionel's **height** is a special **characteristic**. When he was a boy, people noticed he was very **short**. He did not **get** taller. He had to take medicine. It helped him and he got taller. He is five feet, seven inches **tall**. He is not very tall! But his height is not a problem. People **notice** his skill. He gets a lot of attention. He is a famous soccer player. People all over the world know him.

Stop and Think

Read the questions in the first paragraph. What do you think? Is a skill something you get from your parents or something you learn?

Grammar in the Readings

Notice *we* + verbs in the reading.

Use *we* + verbs to tell about you and one or more people.

> **We have** long legs.   *we* = the writer and her family

Notice *they* + verbs in the reading.

Use *they* + verbs to tell about two or more people.

> **They wanted** him on their team.   *they* = the coaches

GO ONLINE
for grammar practice

Check Your Understanding

C. Use words from the text to complete the sentences.

1. People think Lionel Messi is the _best soccer player in the world_ .

2. Tell about Lionel's family members: He has two _____ and

   _____ .

3. He was very good. Coaches _____ his skill.

4. Many people noticed Lionel's height. When he was a boy, he was

   _____ .

5. He had to take medicine. The medicine helped him. He got

   _____ .

D. Answer the questions. Use your own ideas.

1. Why do you think Lionel Messi is great at soccer? _____

   _____

2. How can people get better at something? _____

   _____

Vocabulary Strategy: Collocations with *get*

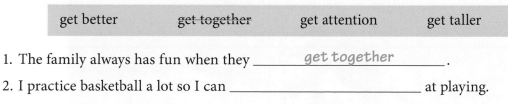

Recycle

the Vocabulary Strategy

E. Read the text on page 26 again. Check the words the writer uses after the verb *get*.

1. _____ soccer

2. _____ skill

3. _____ attention

4. _____ short

5. _____ taller

F. Complete each sentence with a collocation from the box.

get better	~~get together~~	get attention	get taller

1. The family always has fun when they _____ get together _____ .

2. I practice basketball a lot so I can _____ at playing.

3. When children grow, they _____ .

4. We _____ because we are very tall.

Reading Strategy: Find the Topic

G. Answer the questions.

1. Look at the title and read the first sentence. Write the words that are in both the title and the first sentence.

   Lionel Messi _____

2. Look at words that are repeated (used again and again) in the first paragraph. The word *soccer* is used four times. Write another word from the first paragraph that is also repeated.

   _____

3. What is the first paragraph about? _____

   _____

4. Write two words that are repeated two times in the second paragraph.

   _____

5. What does the second paragraph talk about? _____

   _____

6. Read the title. Look at your answers for questions 1–5. What is the topic?

   _____

7. Write a caption for the photograph of Lionel Messi. _____

   _____

   _____

● Make Connections: Text to Text

A. Think about the two texts. Circle the best answer.

1. Both texts are about _____ .

   a. a person and his or her family   b. the greatest people

2. The texts are different. In _____ , the writer describes herself.

   a. "How Am I Like My Family?"   b. "Who Is Lionel Messi?"

3. In _____ , the writer is writing about someone famous.

   a. "How Am I Like My Family?"   b. "Who Is Lionel Messi?"

B. Compare the two readings. On the left, write words from Reading 1. On the right, write words from Reading 2. Write words from both readings in the middle.

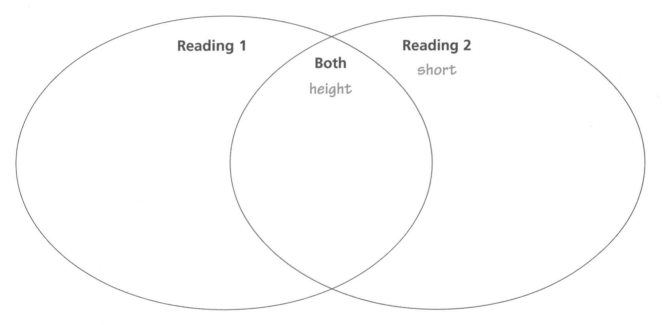

Reading 1

Both

height

Reading 2

short

C. Read each phrase. Does it go with Reading 1, Reading 2, or both texts? Write _1, 2,_ or _both_.

1. __1__ have a big family

2. _____ a special characteristic

3. _____ had to take medicine

4. _____ plays soccer

5. _____ gets a lot of attention

6. _____ family member

7. _____ people notice

AFTER READING

Summarizing and Retelling

A. Complete the sentences with the words from the box. Then read the paragraphs to a partner to summarize.

Adjectives	Nouns	Verbs
short tall	characteristics family height members	get notice

1.   In "How Am I Like My Family?" the writer tells about the _____ she

shares with her _____. She is _____, and she has red

hair. People _____ her.

2.   In "Who Is Lionel Messi?" the writer tells about a great soccer player and his

family. When Lionel was a boy, people saw that he was very _____.

He took medicine and got taller. Now people don't notice his _____.

They see his great skill.

3.   In both texts, the writer talks about a person and his or her family

_____. The writers talk about characteristics. They discuss questions:

What characteristics do people have? How do you _____ better at

something?

B. Write a short answer to each question.

1. What characteristics did the writer of "How Am I Like My Family?" write about?

_____

2. What characteristics did the writer of "Who Is Lionel Messi?" write about?

_____

3. Look back at the pictures and texts on pages 24 and 26. Answer the questions below. Look at the Oxford 2000 keywords on page 133 and find five words to help you.

   a. What other characteristics does the writer of "How Am I Like My Family?" have?

   _____

   b. What other characteristics does Lionel Messi have?

   _____

Word Partners

family name

family dinner

family tree

family vacation

family portrait

GO ONLINE
to practice
word partners

● Make Connections: Text to World

A. Think about the two texts. Circle the best answer.

1. What do the writers want you to do?

   a. think about your family and characteristics

   b. play soccer

   c. have people notice you

2. Who might want to read these texts?

   a. people who are interested in people

   b. people with red hair

   c. family members

3. Why did the writers write "How Am I Like My Family?" and "Who Is Lionel Messi?"?

   a. to tell about famous people

   b. to tell about people's characteristics

   c. to tell about friends

B. Complete the chart with phrases to answer the questions.

Texts about People

Why do writers tell about people?	
Why do people read about other people?	
What can you learn from texts about people?	

C. Talk with a partner. Who do you like to read about? What characteristics do they have? Look at the Oxford 2000 keywords on page 133 and find five words to help you.

Chant

GO ONLINE for the Chapter 1 Vocabulary & Grammar Chant

CHAPTER 2

Who Are Your Friends?

- Short o /ɑ/ sound
- Use examples to find word meanings
- Identify main idea and details
- *I am (not)* + adjectives; *I* + verbs

▲ BEFORE READING ▸ Oxford 2000 🔑 words to talk about friendship

Learn Vocabulary

A. Look at the pictures and read the sentences.

1. **Friends** are people you like. You **share** many things with friends.

2. People form **friendships**. Many people **form** friendships with the people they live next to.

3. Friends have **common interests**. They like the same things.

4. **Friendly** people have **conversations**. They talk with many people.

B. Complete each sentence with a word from the box.

common	friends	friendships	interests
conversations	friendly	form	share

1. Many people _____ *form* _____ friendships with other students in their class.

2. I have _____ on my soccer team. We like playing together.

3. My sister and I have _____ interests. We like biking, running, and studying.

4. My friend Junyi and I _____ many interests. We both drink tea, read books, and watch movies.

5. I have lots of _____ each day. I talk to my mom, my teacher, and my friends.

6. My friends from school all have common _____. We love art and Spanish class.

7. My teacher is very _____. She smiles and says hello to all the students in the school.

8. At my school, they plan fun things. The teachers want us to form _____ with the other students.

C. Match each interest to the correct picture.

cooking	~~reading~~	sports	travel

1. reading

2. _____

3. _____

4. _____

GO ONLINE for more practice

D. Discuss the pictures in Activity C with a partner. What interests do you share?

Preview the Text

E. Look at the pictures and text on page 36. Circle the correct answer.

1. Who do you think the people in the photos are?

   a. family members   b. friends   c. workers

2. What do you think the topic of the text is?

   a. happiness   b. friendship   c. school

3. Where do you think this text is from?

   a. an advertisement   b. an email   c. a magazine

4. What idea do you think the writer does NOT talk about?

   a. conversation   b. being happy   c. different jobs

5. Read the caption below the pictures. How do the men know each other?

   a. They are co-workers.   b. They are friends.   c. They are family members.

Sounds of English

Spelling Connection

A. Listen to the word *box*. What sound does the *o* make? Circle four words below that have the same sound as in *box*. Listen for /ɑ/.

     lot   hot   robot   note   not   alone

B. Circle the vocabulary words that have the short o sound as in *box*.

     common   conversation   cooking

     form   sports   travel

C. These words are in the text on page 36. Circle the word with the short o sound as in *box*.

     often   show   people   other

● Make Connections: Text to Self

A. Answer the questions.

1. Where do your friends live? _____

_____

2. What do you do with your friends? _____

_____

3. When do you see your friends? _____

_____

4. When do you have conversations with new people? _____

_____

5. Where do people's friendships form? _____

_____

B. Think about your friends. Complete the chart.

Name of Friend	What common interests do you share?	How did your friendship form?
Jonathan	soccer, art, reading	He lives close to me.

C. Think about friendships. Why do you think friendships form? Number the ideas from *1* to *8* to show what you think are the most important reasons.

_____ People like conversations.

_____ Friends make each other happy.

_____ People see each other a lot and become friends.

_____ People share a common interest.

_____ People live close to each other.

_____ People work together.

_____ People want to be with other people.

_____ People see each other every day at the store or another place.

🔊 Reading 1

A. Look at groups of words. Move your eye to the right. Read another group of words and move on. Do not stop after each word.

Who are your friends? | Do you share | common interests?

B. Now read the text on your own.

Forming Friendships

Who are your **friends**? Do you **share common interests**? Do you and your friends like to read or watch sports? Do you run together? Many times, friends like the same things. It is fun to do things together. Sharing activities helps friends feel close. Maybe you and your friend just like talking.

These men lived in houses next to each other when they were boys. They lived in the same neighborhood for a long time.

Conversation is very important to friendships. People need other people. In fact, people with friends live longer than people without friends. Friends make people happy.

Why do **friendships form**? People think they form because of common interests. Most often, people become friends because they live near each other. Friendships also form because people go to work or school together. We think that we choose our friends because we share interests. This isn't always true. People see each other a lot, and they become friends. For example, you sit next to someone at work. You speak to that person every day. Or you see someone in your neighborhood. Then you become **friendly**. Friends aren't the people who are most like us. They are the people we see a lot. They live and work near us.

Check Your Understanding

C. Circle the best answer to complete each sentence.

1. Friendships form because you _____.

   a. have an interest in the person

   b. live, work, or go to school with the person

   c. play sports

2. People with friends _____ .

    a. live longer

    b. are more friendly

    c. have more interests

3. People think that they _____ their friends.

    a. meet

    b. choose

    c. like

4. This text tells _____ .

    a. how to make friends

    b. how to be friendly

    c. why people become friends

Vocabulary Strategy

Use Examples to Find Word Meanings

You can find examples in a text to help you understand word meanings.

*I am friends with my **neighbors**. For example, Jonathan and I live on the same street. We talk every day.*

What is the example of the word *neighbor*?

Jonathan and I live on the same street.

This example shows the meaning of *neighbors*.

GO ONLINE
for more
practice

D. Read the sentences from the text. Answer the questions.

1. "Do you share common interests? Do you and your friends like to read or watch sports? Do you run together?"

    What are the examples of *interests*? _____ read, watch sports, run _____

2. "Many times, friends like the same things. It is fun to do things together. Sharing activities helps friends feel close. Maybe you and your friend just like talking."

    What is an example of an *activity*? _____

3. "People see each other a lot, and they become friends. For example, you sit next to someone at work."

    What is an example of the phrase *see each other*? _____

Identify Main Idea and Details

Each paragraph has a main idea. Identifying the main idea helps you understand the important information. The other sentences are the details. Details support the main idea and add information.

Use these strategies to help you find the main idea.

1. Read the title. Read the first paragraph.

2. Find the sentence you think is the most important. Ask, "Why did the writer write this paragraph?"

3. Read the other sentences. Do they explain the main idea or add more information? These are the details.

GO ONLINE
for more
practice

E. Look at the text on page 36. Circle the correct answer.

1. How many paragraphs are there?	1	(2)
2. How many main ideas are there?	1	2
3. How many sentences are in the first paragraph?	12	13
4. How many sentences are in the second paragraph?	13	14
5. Which paragraph do you think is the most important?	1	2

F. One of the sentences below is the main idea of the first paragraph of the text on page 36. Label it *MI*. The other sentences are details. Label those *D*.

1. __D__ Maybe you and your friend just like talking.

2. _____ Friends make people happy.

3. _____ Do you run together?

4. _____ In fact, people with friends live longer than people without friends.

G. One of the sentences below is the main idea of the second paragraph of the text on page 36. Label it *MI*. The other sentences are details. Label those *D*.

1. __D__ People think they form because of common interests.

2. _____You see someone in your neighborhood.

3. _____ For example, you sit next to someone at work.

4. _____ People see each other a lot, and they become friends.

◄ Reading 2

A. Preview the text. Then read it on your own.

Do Friends Use Small Talk?

What is small talk? Small talk is a kind of **conversation**. I make small talk when I meet someone. Sometimes, I talk about the weather. I say it is a nice day. I say it is warm outside. Other times, I ask questions. For example, I make small talk in line at the store. I ask the cashier about her day. Small talk is a way to be **friendly**. It helps people feel comfortable. I feel good after making small talk. It makes the other person smile, too. It's a way to be nice.

When you make small talk, you smile. You feel comfortable.

Stop and Think

Make a connection. When do you use small talk?

I read an article about small talk. It does help **friendships form**. But people need to talk about more important things. They want to have meaningful conversations. In a deep, meaningful conversation, you **share** your feelings and your thoughts. You talk about your life. You discuss love and family. Deep conversations make people happy. The more deep conversations a person has, the happier the person becomes. I agree. I am happy when I share my feelings with a **friend**. We might talk about sad things. The conversation is important. It has meaning, and that makes us feel good.

Grammar in the Readings

Notice *I am (not)* + adjectives in the reading.

Use *I am* to tell what is true about you.

I am happy when I share my feelings with a friend.

Use *I am not* to tell what is not true about you.

I am not happy in the early morning.

Notice *I* + verbs in the reading.

Use *I* + verbs to tell what you do.

I make small talk. I talk about the weather.

GO ONLINE
for grammar practice

Check Your Understanding

B. Use a phrase from the text on page 39 to answer each question.

1. What is small talk? _____ *a kind of conversation* _____

2. How does small talk help make people feel? _____

3. Who does the writer make small talk with? _____

4. What do people talk about in deep conversations? _____

5. What kind of conversation makes people happy? _____

C. Think about the text on page 39. Check the questions that are good for small talk.

1. _____ What are you studying?

2. _____ What do you think is most important in life?

3. _____ Where are you from?

4. _____ What languages do you speak?

5. _____ Why are you upset?

Recycle

the Vocabulary
Strategy

Vocabulary Strategy: Use Examples to Find Word Meanings

D. Look for the underlined word or phrase in the text on page 39. Circle the example of the underlined word or phrase.

1. What is an example of small talk?

   a. I meet someone.

   b. I say it is warm outside.

   c. I wait in line at the store.

2. What is an example of being nice?

   a. I help someone.

   b. I talk about the things I want.

   c. I feel good.

3. What is an example of a meaningful conversation?

   a. I talk about my thoughts.

   b. I make small talk.

   c. I talk about soccer.

4. What is an example of sharing feelings?

   a. I talk about the weather.

   b. I talk about my life.

   c. I go to the movies.

E. Read each description. Circle the meaning of the underlined word.

1. I talk to the cashier at the store. Paulo tells me how much to pay. He also makes jokes. He makes me smile.

   a. person who makes someone smile

   b. person who works at a store

   c. person who you talk to

2. I talk to my co-worker. Helena sits in the desk next to me at work.

   a. person you work with

   b. person you sit by

   c. person you share a desk with

3. I see my son's <u>teacher</u> at school. Mrs. Chen is a great teacher and fun to talk to.

   a. person who is great

   b. person who teaches at a school

   c. person who you study with

4. I eat lunch at the same restaurant every day. I talk to the <u>waiter</u> when he brings me my food. We talk every day. We are friends.

   a. person who you are friends with

   b. person who you eat food with

   c. person who works at a restaurant

Reading Strategy: Identify Main Idea and Details

Recycle

the Reading Strategy

F. One of the sentences below is the main idea of the first paragraph of the text on page 39. Label it *MI*. The other sentences are details. Label those *D*.

1. __D__ I say it is a nice day.

2. _____ It's a way to be kind.

3. _____ Small talk is a kind of conversation.

4. _____ I feel good after making small talk.

G. One of the sentences below is the main idea of the second paragraph of the text on page 39. Label it *MI*. The other sentences are details. Label those *D*.

1. _____ You talk about your life.

2. _____ I agree.

3. _____ You discuss love and family.

4. _____ Deep conversations make people happy.

⬤ Make Connections: Text to Text

A. Read each phrase. Does it describe Reading 1, Reading 2, or both? Write the phrase in the Venn diagram.

uses *I* + verb statements	uses examples
talks about friendship	talks about two kinds of conversation
explains how something forms	tells what research shows

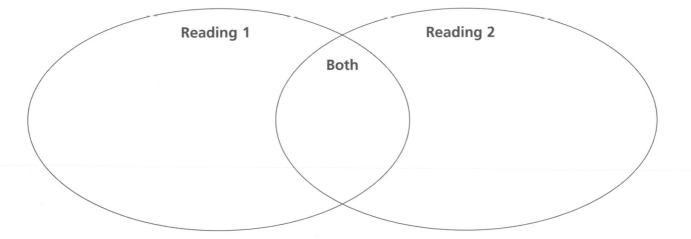

Reading 1   Reading 2

Both

Summarizing and Retelling

A. Complete the questions with the words from the box. Some of the words have to be changed to fit the sentences. For example, *friendship* **has to be changed to** *friendships.* **Then read the questions to a partner to retell the ideas.**

Adjectives	Nouns	Verbs
common friendly	conversation friend friendship interest	form share

1. Why do people become _____?

2. Do _____ form because you live close?

3. Do friendships form because you share a(n) _____?

4. Does being _____ help friendships form?

5. What do you say in _____ when you make small talk?

6. What do you _____ in conversations with your friends?

7. How do friendships _____?

8. Do friends have _____ interests?

B. Now write the numbers of the questions from Activity A that each text answers in the chart below.

Reading 1	Reading 2	Both

Word Partners

show interest

express interest

lose interest

develop an interest

GO ONLINE
to practice
word partners

● Make Connections: Text to World

A. Think about the two texts. Check the statements you agree with.

"Forming Friendships"

1. _____ Friends share common interests.

2. _____ Friends live close to each other.

3. _____ Friends make people happy.

4. _____ People meet their friends at work or school.

5. _____ People need people to talk to.

"Do Friends Use Small Talk?"

6. _____ It's nice to make small talk.

7. _____ Small talk makes people feel good.

8. _____ Small talk helps friendships form.

9. _____ Friends have meaningful conversations.

10. _____ People are happy to talk about their feelings.

B. Compare your answers from Activity A with a partner. Tell why you agree or disagree. Look at the Oxford 2000 keywords on page 133 and find five words to help you.

I do not agree with the writer of "Forming Friendships." I think …

I do not agree with the writer of "Do Friends Use Small Talk?" I think …

I agree with the writer of "Forming Friendships." I think …

I agree with the writer of "Do Friends Use Small Talk?" I think …

Chant

GO ONLINE for the Chapter 2 Vocabulary & Grammar Chant

Why Do We Like Art?

- /ʊ/ **sound**
- **Identify synonyms**
- **Make inferences**
- *he/she/it is (not)* + adjectives; *he/she/it* + verbs

▲ BEFORE READING ▶ Oxford 2000 🔑 words to talk about art

Learn Vocabulary

A. Match each picture to the correct sentence.

_____ I like **real** flowers.

_____ I have a **painting** of trees in a forest.

_____ At the beach, you **look** at the ocean.

___1___ There are many **colors** in the sunset.

1.

2.

3.

4.

B. Match each picture to the correct sentence.

_____ The Burj Khalifa is a **famous** building.

___1___ She **appears** happy at school.

_____ I **describe** the problem to the doctor.

_____ I am next to the **person** in the green coat.

1.

2.

3.

4.

C. Complete each sentence with a word from the box.

appears	describe	look	person
color	famous	painting	real

1. The lake _____appears_____ blue.

2. I have an orange tree, but it is not _____ .

3. I can _____ the book. It is about a famous family in China. It's very good.

4. My favorite _____ is a picture of my mother. My grandfather painted it.

5. The _____ next to me is my sister.

6. I _____ out the window in my room a lot. There is a forest outside.

7. The Eiffel Tower is _____ . Many people go to Paris to see it.

8. Is the _____ of stop signs always red?

Oxford 2000 🔑

Use the Oxford 2000 list on page 133 to find more words to describe the pictures on these pages. Share your words with a partner.

GO ONLINE
for more practice

Preview the Text

D. Look at the picture on page 48. Answer the questions.

1. What is in this painting? _____

2. Describe the painting. _____

_____

E. Look at the text on page 48. Circle the best answer.

1. Who do you think this text is for?

   a. people who study math and science

   b. people who read the news

   c. people who like art

2. What do you think the text does?

   a. describe the painting

   b. explain how to paint

   c. describe the artist

3. What do you think is the topic of the text?

   a. a person named Mona Lisa

   b. different famous paintings

   c. the *Mona Lisa*

Sounds of English

Spelling Connection

🔊 A. Listen to the word *book*. What sound does the *oo* make? The sound /ʊ/ can be spelled with *oo* or *u*. Circle four words below that have the same sound as in *book*. Listen for /ʊ/.

took   good   put   nut   foot

B. Circle the vocabulary word that has the same sound as in *book*.

color   famous   look   person

● Make Connections: Text to Self

A. Write a short answer to each question.

1. The painting on page 48 is famous because _____

2. I like/don't like the painting because _____

3. Why do people like paintings? _____

4. What art do you like? _____

B. Describe each painting to a partner using the words in the box. Say what you like.

| blue | orange | purple | yellow | green | pink | red |

1.

2.

C. Think about a painting or photo you like. Complete the chart.

Questions	Answers
Who is in the painting or photo?	
How does the person appear?	
Does the person look real? Why or why not?	
What colors are in it?	
How would you describe it?	
What makes the painting or photo special?	

▲▲ DURING READING
▶ Vocabulary strategy: Identify synonyms
▶ Reading strategy: Make inferences

◉ Reading 1

A. When we read, we focus on the most important words. We focus on the nouns and verbs.

The most famous <u>painting</u> in the <u>world</u> <u>measures</u> 20 by 30 <u>inches</u>.

B. Now read the text on your own.

Why Is the *Mona Lisa* Famous?

The most **famous** painting in the world measures 20 by 30 inches. It is a well-known portrait of a woman. The *Mona Lisa* hangs in Paris. It is from the early 1500s. A woman's dark brown eyes **appear** to look at you. There is a small smile on her lips. She looks happy. Many people **describe** the **painting** as interesting because her eyes appear to follow you. But why is it so famous? First, the painter is the great Leonardo da Vinci. Second, the portrait was painted to a human scale. It is about the same size as a **real person**.

Detail from the Mona Lisa *by Leonardo da Vinci*

The portrait is special because da Vinci's painting was not like his others. The *Mona Lisa* was different. The portrait shows the woman. You see the dark **colors** of her hair, eyes, and clothes. But it also shows the background. Behind her, there is a road. There are trees and a lake. You see the woman. She appears to be at peace. Then you **look** out to the trees and the land in the distance. The natural world is outside. This is why the painting is famous. You see the beautiful view. Look back at the woman. And she smiles at you. It appears a real person is in front of you.

Stop and Think

What words are important?

Check Your Understanding

C. Circle the best answer to complete each sentence.

1. The painting is interesting because _____.

   a. Leonardo da Vinci is in it   (b.) the eyes appear to follow you

2. Leonardo da Vinci _____ the *Mona Lisa*.

   a. painted   b. wrote

3. The portrait is _____ .

    a. very big   b. human size

4. The painting shows _____ .

    a. the woman   b. the woman and nature

5. The *Mona Lisa* was _____ other paintings by
Leonardo da Vinci.

    a. the same as   b. different from

Vocabulary Strategy

Identify Synonyms

Synonyms are words that have similar meanings. Using synonyms can make a text more interesting. For example, writers use synonyms so they don't repeat the same word. Identifying synonyms can help you understand a text more easily. Look at the two sentences below. The synonyms appear in bold.

                verb   verb

*The painting **looks** beautiful. The painting **appears** beautiful.*

Notice that the synonyms are the same part of speech: verbs. Synonyms can be nouns, verbs, or adjectives.

GO ONLINE
for more
practice

D. Circle the synonym in the second sentence for the underlined word in the first sentence.

1. I have a <u>huge</u> painting that covers my wall. It is a big picture of my house.

2. My sister painted my eyes very <u>small</u>. They looked very little.

3. The portrait is very <u>pretty</u>. The woman looks beautiful.

4. The cake tastes <u>very good</u>. It is wonderful.

5. My sister gets <u>scared</u> at night. She is frightened of the dark.

E. Circle the synonym in the second sentence for the underlined word in the first sentence.

1. The most <u>famous</u> painting in the world measures 20 by 30 inches.

    It is a well-known portrait of a woman.

2. Second, the portrait was painted to a human <u>scale</u>.

    It is about the same size as a real person.

3. Second, the portrait was painted to a <u>human</u> scale.

    It is about the same size as a real person.

Reading Strategy

Make Inferences

An inference is a guess you make. Sometimes a text gives you some information that helps you make a guess about something not in the text. Inferences help you make connections.

1. Making inferences can help you understand the text: Was the *Mona Lisa* similar to da Vinci's other paintings? The writer does not describe da Vinci's other paintings. But the text says, "The portrait is special because da Vinci's painting was not like his others."

   Inference: *Da Vinci's other paintings did not include a person and the background in the distance.*

2. You can make inferences to understand word meanings. The writer says, "You see the woman. She appears to be at peace." What does *at peace* mean? The text also says that the woman smiles and looks happy.

   Inference: *I think* at peace *means she is calm and happy.*

GO ONLINE
for more
practice

F. Match each statement from the text to an inference.

1. ___*b*___ But why is it so famous? First, the painter is the great Leonardo da Vinci.

2. _____ Many people describe the painting as interesting because her eyes appear to follow you.

3. _____ You see the woman. She appears to be at peace. Then you look out to the trees and the land in the distance. The natural world is outside. This is why the painting is famous.

4. _____ Second, the portrait was painted to a human scale. It is about the same size as a real person.

5. _____ But it also shows the background. Behind her, there is a road.

Inferences

a. The size of the painting is important. It makes the person appear real.

b. ~~Many people liked and admired Leonardo da Vinci.~~

c. People like to see nature in paintings. It shows peace and calm.

d. The eyes make the painting well known.

e. The background is the part of the painting that is behind the subject.

◉ Reading 2

A. Preview the text. Then read it to yourself.

Picasso's Portraits

People like paintings for different reasons. What do you think makes a portrait **famous**? Is it because the **person** in the **painting** is famous? Or is it because the portrait **looks real**? Does it show how the artist feels about the person? How important are the **colors**? One person loves a painting. Another person does not like it. So how does a painting become **famous**? Often paintings become popular because the painter did something new.

Picasso liked to look at objects from history, such as African masks.

In the past, artists painted portraits to appear real. In the early 1900s, Picasso painted a portrait to explore the shapes of objects. Picasso went to Spain. He liked the art there. He began to paint faces differently. He painted faces as masks. His portrait of Gertrude Stein is very famous. Picasso looked at Ms. Stein. Then he painted the body. You see her white shirt. You see her black coat. They look real. But he painted the head when she was not there. He painted her face as a mask. It does not appear real. It looks different. It is interesting. Sometimes an artist does something new. This makes people think differently. And we ask questions: *What is art? What makes something beautiful?*

Stop and Think

Think about the writer's questions. Stop to answer. Then read the text again.

Grammar in the Readings

Notice *he/she/it is (not)* + adjectives in the readings.

He is for a male. *She* is for a female. *It* is for an object, place, or thing.

Use *he/she/it is* + adjective to tell about a person or thing.

  Look at the painting. **It is** *different..*

Use *he/she/it is not* + adjective to tell what is not true about a person or thing.

  Look at the painting. **It is not** *beautiful.*

Notice *he/she/it* + verbs in the readings.

Use *he/she/it* + verbs to tell what a person or thing does.

  Picasso went to Spain. **He liked** *the art there.*

GO ONLINE
for grammar practice

Check Your Understanding

B. Circle the correct answer.

1. Which question does the writer answer in the first paragraph?

    a. What makes a painter interesting?   (b.) How does a painting become famous?

2. What made Picasso paint his portrait differently?

    a. his trip to Spain   b. the woman in the painting

3. What is true of the portrait?

    a. The face looks like a mask.   b. The face looks real.

4. What did Picasso do that was new?

    a. He went to Spain.   b. He painted the face as a mask.

5. What does the writer NOT discuss about the painting?

    a. the colors   b. who Gertrude Stein is

Recycle

the Vocabulary
Strategy

Vocabulary Strategy: Identify Synonyms

C. Circle the synonym in sentence b for the underlined word in sentence a.

1. a. So how does a painting become <u>famous</u>?

    b. Often paintings become (popular) because the painter did something new.

2. a. Some portraits don't <u>appear</u> real.

    a. The man in the portrait seems to be smiling.

3. a. Many people like to look at <u>art</u>.

    b. Looking at paintings makes people think differently.

4. a. Paintings become famous because the painter did something <u>new</u>.

    b. The way Picasso painted was different.

5. a. People often visit <u>museums</u> to see art.

    b. These places have paintings and objects from the past.

Recycle

the Reading
Strategy

Reading Strategy: Make Inferences

D. Match each statement from the text to an inference.

1. __c__ Picasso went to Spain. He liked the art there. He began to paint faces differently. He painted faces as masks.

2. _____ Often paintings become popular because the painter did something new.

3. _____ In the early 1900s, Picasso painted a portrait to explore the shapes of objects.

4. _____ In the past, artists painted portraits to appear real.

Inferences

a. Doing something new is important in art.

b. To explore something is to think about it and try something out.

c. ~~In Spain, Picasso saw masks.~~

d. Artists don't always follow other artists from the past.

E. Answer the questions.

1. Write a sentence from the text. _____

2. Read the sentence. What do you think is true? Make an inference. _____

_____

⬤ Make Connections: Text to Text

A. Think about the two texts. Fill in the chart with the phrases from the box.

painted the view behind the portrait	painted the face as a mask
a woman named Gertrude Stein	Leonardo da Vinci
talks about the painter's interests	talks about colors, nature, and eyes
Pablo Picasso	a smiling woman and the background

Questions	"Why Is the *Mona Lisa* Famous?"	"Picasso's Portraits"
What is the painting of?		
Who is the painter?		
What did the painter do that was new?		
What does the text describe?		

B. Why are the *Mona Lisa* and Pablo Picasso's portraits famous? What characteristics do both portraits share? Use the words in the box to help you.

real	person	appears	looks	new

The portraits are famous because _____

_____

Summarizing and Retelling

A. Look at the words from this chapter. Circle the correct word to complete each sentence. Then read the paragraphs to a partner to summarize.

Adjectives	Nouns	Verbs
famous real	colors painting person	appear describe look

1.   The *Mona Lisa* is a famous *painting* / *person*. The woman's eyes *describe* / *appear* to

    look at you. The painting shows a woman and the view behind her. Many of the

    colors / *real* are dark.

2.   Picasso's portrait is of a *color* / *person*. Her name is Gertrude Stein. Her face

    appears as a mask. The writer *describes* / *appears* how Picasso painted the portrait.

3.   In both texts, the writer describes why the painting is *colors* / *famous*. In the *Mona*

    Lisa, the woman *looks* / *describes* real. Gertrude Stein's portrait is different. Her face

    doesn't appear *famous* / *real*.

Word Partners

look forward to

look into

look out of

look at

_____

GO ONLINE
to practice
word partners

B. What do you think? Use the words from the box in Activity A to describe the paintings.

The *Mona Lisa*	*Portrait of Gertrude Stein*

● Make Connections: Text to World

A. Think about the two texts. Answer the questions.

1. Why do paintings become famous?

_____

_____

_____

2. Why do writers write about paintings?

_____

_____

_____

3. What do writers describe when they write about a painting?

_____

_____

_____

B. What do you think makes a portrait beautiful? Check the statements you agree with.

1. _____ The colors are very important.

2. _____ The person in the portrait is famous.

3. _____ The painter does something new.

4. _____ The portrait appears real.

5. _____ The painter paints the background behind the person.

6. _____ The person in the portrait looks at you.

C. Compare your answers from Activity B with a partner. Tell why you agree or disagree. Look at the Oxford 2000 keywords on page 133 and find five words to help you.

Chant

GO ONLINE
for the
Chapter 3
Vocabulary &
Grammar Chant

Look at the word bank for Unit 1. Check (✓) the words you know.
Circle the words you want to learn better.

OXFORD 2000 🔑		
Adjectives	**Nouns**	**Verbs**
common	characteristic	appear
famous	color	describe
friendly	conversation	form
real	family	get
short	friend	look
tall	friendship	notice
	height	share
	interest	
	member	
	painting	
	person	

PRACTICE WITH THE OXFORD 2000 🔑

A. Use the words in the chart. Match adjectives with nouns.

1. _____real person_____   2. _____

3. _____   4. _____

5. _____

B. Use the words in the chart. Match verbs with nouns.

1. _____notice a friend_____   2. _____

3. _____   4. _____

5. _____

C. Use the words in the chart. Match verbs with adjective noun partners.

1. _describe common characteristics_   2. _____

3. _____   4. _____

5. _____

UNIT 2 Places

CHAPTER 4 What Can We Explore?

- Short a /æ/ sound
- Words with multiple meanings
- Use pictures
- *there is/there are* + nouns; pronouns *it* and *they*

▲ BEFORE READING ► Oxford 2000 🔑 words to talk about exploring

Learn Vocabulary

A. Look at the pictures and read the sentences.

1. The **land** is the earth under your feet. It is not water.

   The land around my house is green and beautiful.

2. **Distance** is how far one place is from another place.

   The distance from the Earth to the moon is 238,900 miles!

3. A **planet** is a large object in the sky. A planet moves around the sun or other stars.

   Planet Earth is our home.

4. The **ocean** is salt water.

   There are five oceans.

B. Complete each sentence with a word from the box.

~~distance~~	land	ocean	planet

1. I have to travel a long _____*distance*_____ to visit my family.

2. Neptune is the farthest _____ from the sun.

3. My sister's house is on the beach near the _____.

4. The _____ in a desert can be dry and sandy.

C. Match each description to the correct picture.

1. A **map** shows the land. It's a picture of where things are.

   I have a map of the city.

2. When you **explore** something, you learn about it.

   I like to explore the woods by my house.

3. **Percent** shows one part of a hundred.

   Sixty percent of the students in the school are women.

4. **Size** is how big or small something is.

   These balls are all different sizes.

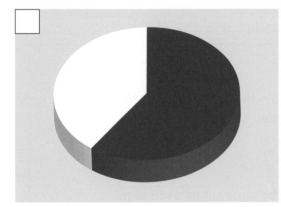

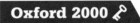

Oxford 2000

Use the Oxford 2000 list on page 133 to find more words to describe the pictures on these pages. Share your words with a partner.

1

river

street

plaza

park

GO ONLINE for more practice

Preview the Text

D. Look at the pictures on page 62. Write a short answer to each question.

1. Why do you think there is a picture of penguins in Antarctica? _____

_____

2. Why do you think there is a picture of a satellite? _____

_____

3. What percent of the world do you think is ocean? _____

_____

4. What percent of the world do you think we have maps for? _____

_____

E. Look at the text on page 62. Write a short answer to each question.

1. Look at the title. What do you think the writer will describe? _____

_____

2. Read the first sentence. Write an answer to the question. _____

_____

Sounds of English

Spelling Connection

🔊 A. Listen to the word *man*. What sound does the *a* make? Circle three words below that have the same sound as in *man*. Listen for /æ/.

    paper   can   apple   name   path

B. Circle the vocabulary words that have the same sound as in *man*.

    land   ocean   planet   map   explore   size

C. These words are in the text on page 62. Circle three words that have the /æ/ sound as in *man*.

    satellite   had   distance   name   cameras

● Make Connections: Text to Self

A. Think about the topic of the reading on page 62. Answer the questions.

1. Circle the kinds of maps you use.

   city   subway   country   world   building

2. When do you use maps?

   in a new place   on the train   in the car

3. Describe another time when you use a map. _____

   _____

4. Write four different things maps show. _____

   _____

   _____

5. These places are mentioned in the reading. Find them on a map or globe. Which one do you want to explore?

   South America   Antarctica   Australia

6. How do you learn about the world? Circle the things you do.

   look at photos   look at maps   read books   read online (Internet)

   travel   talk to others   listen to news   go to school

B. Why do we explore our world? What can we learn? Write questions in the chart.

How deep is the ocean?

Exploring Our World
What questions do we try to answer?

Question Words
Who
What
Where
When
Why
How

◉ Reading 1

A. Look for the numbers in the text. Say them. Then read the text on your own.

Exploring Earth

Stop and Think

What does the writer describe?

How much of the world do we know? In 2006, Google had **maps** of 37 **percent** of the world. Satellites took these pictures. They show the **land** and people from high above the Earth. In 2012, there were maps of 75 percent of land on Earth. Then Google Maps added more pictures. Cameras in cars took pictures of city streets. In 2007, five cities had these pictures. In 2012, 3,000 cities in 35 countries had these pictures. You can **explore** every place on land. You can see pictures from the coldest place on Earth. The street pictures in Antarctica show penguins!

We have many maps of the land. **Oceans** cover 70 percent of the world. Ninety-five percent of the ocean is very, very deep. It's a big **distance**. Now, Google Maps is taking pictures of the ocean. There are pictures of the Great Barrier Reef in Australia. There are pictures of underwater mountains near South America. Scientists are learning about the ocean with Google Maps. Now people can explore underwater worlds from their homes!

Satellites take pictures from high above the Earth.

"Street" views in Antarctica even show penguins!

Check Your Understanding

B. Circle the correct answer.

1. There   *are*   *(are not)*   maps of every place on Earth.

2. There   *are*   *are not*   pictures of the ocean.

3. People   *can*   *cannot*   explore the ocean from their homes.

4. In 2006, there   *were*   *were not*   maps of 75 percent of the world.

5. Satellites   *take*   *do not take*   pictures.

Words with Multiple Meanings

The same word can have different forms. Some words can be nouns or verbs. The meanings are often similar, so learning the different forms can help you build your vocabulary quickly. Nouns that name objects or things often have *a/an* or *the* before them. Verbs tell what the nouns do.

noun

*Do we have **maps** of the world?*

verb

*We can **map** the world using satellites.*

GO ONLINE
for more
practice

C. Read each sentence. Is the underlined word a noun or a verb?

1. They show the <u>land</u> and people from high above the Earth.   (noun)   verb
2. In 1969, humans <u>landed</u> on the moon.   noun   verb
3. Draw a big <u>circle</u> on your paper.   noun   verb
4. <u>Circle</u> the correct answer.   noun   verb
5. The oceans <u>cover</u> 70 percent of the world.   noun   verb
6. The book <u>cover</u> is red.   noun   verb

Reading Strategy

Use Pictures

Writers show information with pictures. A picture can be a photograph or an illustration.

Pictures show how something looks. They show the meaning of ideas in a text. Pictures can also support the text. The pictures in a reading can help you learn more information about the topic.

A photograph is made by a camera. Captions tell what the photograph is of or give more information.

An illustration is a drawing. It can show information. The words are called labels.

Google uses satellites to help create maps.

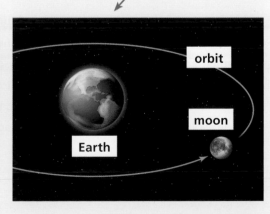

GO ONLINE
for more
practice

D. Look at the pictures on page 62. Answer the questions.

1. What does the writer say about the first photograph in the text? _____

_____

2. What does the writer say about the second photograph in the text? _____

_____

🔊 Reading 2

A. Listen and read along.

What Do We Know about Our Solar System?

The picture below shows our solar system. Textbooks often have this picture. It teaches the names of the **planets**. It shows that the planets orbit the sun. They move in a circle. It also teaches the order of the planets from the sun. Earth is the third planet from the sun. The picture also shows other objects in space. But a satellite did not take this picture and it is not a **map**. It doesn't show everything. There are 170 moons in our solar system! There are also more than 2,500 satellites.

Our Solar System

The picture is helpful, but it can't explain everything. The picture can't show **size** or **distance**. In the picture, the sizes of the planets look similar. Everything looks close to each other. The sizes of the planets are very different. More than 1,000 Earths can fit inside Jupiter. The picture can't show this. It also can't show the distance between the planets. Jupiter is 380,000,000 miles from Earth. The distance is too big. It's difficult to show our solar system in a picture on one page. We are still **exploring** our solar system.

Notice *there is/there are* + nouns in the readings.

Use *there is* with singular nouns.

> **There is** a <u>map</u> of **London**.

Use *there are* with plural nouns.

> **There are** <u>pictures</u> of underwater mountains in South America.

Notice pronouns *it* and *they* in the readings.

Use the pronoun *it* to refer to singular objects.

> <u>Earth</u> is the third planet from the sun. Oceans cover 70 percent of **it**.

Use *they* to refer to plural objects.

> The <u>planets</u> orbit the sun. **They** move in a circle.

GO ONLINE
for grammar
practice

Check Your Understanding

B. Read the sentences. What can you understand from the picture? What can you understand from the text? Write the sentences in the chart.

~~Jupiter is 380,000,000 miles from Earth.~~	There are 170 moons in our solar system.
the order of the planets	The sizes of the planets are very different.
More than 1,000 Earths can fit inside Jupiter.	

What You Know from the Picture	What You Know from the Text
	Jupiter is 380,000,000 miles from Earth.

Recycle

the Vocabulary Strategy

Vocabulary Strategy: Words with Multiple Meanings

C. Read the first sentence. Circle the sentence where the underlined word has the same meaning.

1. The planets circle the sun.
   a. The table is a circle.
   b. The moon circles the Earth.
2. The picture below shows our solar system.
   a. My brother watches shows on TV all day.
   b. My friend shows me photos of her family.
3. It also shows other objects in space.
   a. We have a lot to learn about outer space.
   b. Write your answer in the space on the page.

Recycle

the Reading Strategy

Reading Strategy: Use Pictures

D. Look at the illustration on page 64. Answer the questions.

1. What is the title?
   a. "Our Solar System"
   b. "The Sun"
2. What does the illustration show?
   a. the planets and the stars
   b. the names of the planets in our solar system
3. What planet is closest to the sun?
   a. Mercury
   b. Earth
4. How many labels are there?
   a. eight
   b. nine
5. Why does the writer show this illustration?
   a. The text describes Earth.
   b. The text describes the solar system.

◗◖ Make Connections: Text to Text

A. Read each sentence. Does it describe Reading 1, Reading 2, or both? Write the sentence in the Venn diagram.

There are many maps of the world. They help us explore.

Maps and pictures cannot show everything.

The writer talks about pictures.

We don't know how big outer space is.

Pictures can be helpful.

There are satellite pictures. These are pictures from space.

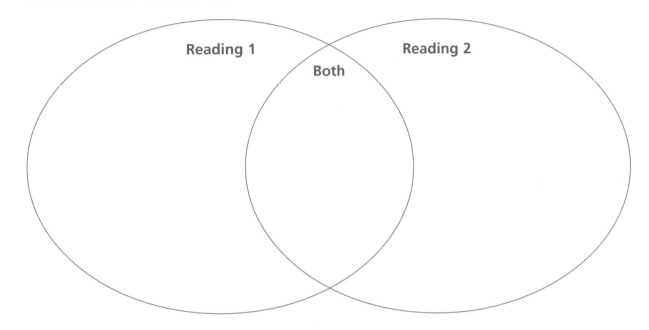

Reading 1 Both Reading 2

B. Both writers use numbers. Match each number to what it describes.

1. _____ More than **1,000** Earths can fit inside Jupiter.   a. percent

2. _____ In 2006, Google had maps of **37** percent of the world.   b. distance

3. _____ By **2012**, there were maps of 75 percent of the world.   c. size

4. _____ Jupiter is **380,000,000** miles from Earth.   d. year

C. Think about why the writers use numbers. Check the reasons.

1. _____ support main idea

2. _____ show interesting detail

3. _____ name a place

4. _____ tell something the picture does not show

5. _____ tell when

Summarizing and Retelling

A. Complete the sentences with the words from the box. Some of the words have to be changed to fit the sentences. For example, *map* has to be changed to *maps*. Then read the paragraphs to a partner to summarize.

Nouns	Verbs
distance land map ocean percent planet size	explore

1.   In the first text, the topic is _____. The writer says that we can use Google Maps to _____ the world. We have pictures from satellites in the sky. They show the _____. He says that there are maps of the land and _____. The ocean covers 70 _____ of Earth, but it's deep and difficult to explore.

2.   In the second text, the writer talks about the _____. He tells the order they are in from the sun. He tells that pictures don't always show the truth. The solar system is so big. It's hard to show the _____ between the planets in an illustration. And it's difficult to show the _____ of the planets.

B. Both writers use pronouns. Find each sentence in the text on page 62 or 64. Circle the word the pronoun refers to.

1. **They** show the land and people from high above the Earth.
   a. pictures   b. planets
2. But a satellite did not take this picture and **it** is not a map.
   a. space   b. picture
3. **It** teaches the names of the planets.
   a. picture   b. solar system
4. **It** also can't show the distance between the planets.
   a. Jupiter   b. picture
5. **They** move in a circle.
   a. planets   b. sun

Word Partners

reach land

live off the land

develop the land

own land

piece of land

GO ONLINE
to practice
word partners

● Make Connections: Text to World

A. Think about texts that explain. Check the statements you agree with.

1. _____ Pictures are helpful, but they can't explain some things.

2. _____ We can learn about our world from photos.

3. _____ Texts are better than pictures and maps at sharing ideas.

4. _____ Pictures can show things that the text cannot.

5. _____ Good writers use pictures or maps to show information.

B. Write ideas that you like to read about in each type of text. Then answer the questions below.

Texts That Explain

Newspapers	Magazines	Textbooks
_____	_____	_____
_____	_____	_____
_____	_____	_____

1. What pictures, maps, or illustrations do you see in these texts?

_____

_____

2. When do writers use numbers in these texts?

_____

_____

3. What words or phrases do writers use when they explain ideas?

_____

_____

4. What information do captions and labels give?

_____

_____

C. Talk about your answers from Activities A and B with a partner. Look at the Oxford 2000 keywords on page 133 and find five words to help you.

Chant

GO ONLINE for the Chapter 4 Vocabulary & Grammar Chant

How Does the World Communicate?

- Short u /ʌ/ sound
- Use a dictionary
- Summarize
- Count and noncount nouns

▲ BEFORE READING ▶ Oxford 2000 🔑 words to talk about communication

Learn Vocabulary

A. Look at the pictures and read the sentences.

1. People learn **languages** to **communicate** with others.

2. People in different **countries speak** different languages.

3. In a **global** world, people use **technology** to communicate their **ideas** to people in other countries.

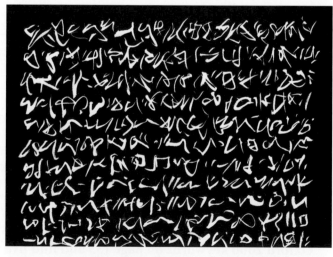

4. Languages **die** when there are no people who know how to speak them.

B. Write each phrase below the correct picture.

| a few people eat | ~~many people watch~~ | a few children play | many children laugh |

1.

_____ many people watch _____

2.

_____

3.

_____

4.

_____

C. Complete the paragraph with the words from the box.

communicate	global	language	technology
~~country~~	ideas	many	speak

People in every _____ country _____ in the world _____ with each

other. This is called _____ communication. People use

_____ to communicate. They share _____ on the

Internet. People need to _____ the same _____.

_____ people learn English. Then they can do business and share ideas.

Oxford 2000 🔑

Use the Oxford 2000 list on page 133 to find more words to describe the pictures on these pages. Share your words with a partner.

GO ONLINE
for more
practice

Preview the Text

D. Look at the text on page 74. Check all the places you might see the text.

1. _____ newspaper   2. _____ textbook   3. _____ book about famous people

4. _____ magazine   5. _____ Internet

E. Look at the picture and text on page 74. Write a short answer to each question.

1. Why do you think the writer shows a picture of a keyboard? _____

_____

2. What language do you think many people use to communicate? _____

_____

3. What language do you think people use to do global business? _____

_____

F. Circle the best answers. There may be more than one for each question.

1. What idea do you think the writer will NOT talk about?

   a. business   b. technology   c. friends

2. Some people speak English as a first language. Make an inference. Who do they learn it from?

   a. parents   b. teachers   c. businesses

3. Some people learn English as a second language. Make an inference. Who do they learn it from?

   a. parents   b. teachers   c. businesses

Sounds of English

Spelling Connection

A. Listen to the word *cup*. What sound does the *u* make? Circle three words below that have the same sound as in *cup*. Listen for /ʌ/. This sound can be spelled with an *o*, *u*, or *ou*.

rude   company   country   quiet   discuss

The letters *ou* also make another sound. The word *count* sounds different from *country*.

B. Circle the vocabulary word that has the /ʌ/ sound as in *cup*.

communicate   country   language   technology

C. These words are in the text on page 74. Circle two words with the short u sound as in *cup*.

study   use   difficult   many

● Make Connections: Text to Self

A. Circle *few* or *many* to answer each question. Remember: *few* means "not many."

1. How many people in the world speak English?	few	(many)
2. How many people use technology to communicate?	few	many
3. How many people in your country speak English?	few	many
4. How many people outside of your country speak your language?	few	many
5. How many people in the world learn English?	few	many

B. Think about the languages you use. Complete the chart.

Questions	Your Answers
1. What languages did you learn from your parents?	
2. What languages do you learn at school?	
3. What language do people use to do business in your country?	
4. What other languages do people speak in your country?	
5. What languages are on websites?	
6. What language do you use with technology?	

C. Check all the things you use English for.

1. _____ to get a job

2. _____ to communicate with people in different countries

3. _____ to read ideas on websites

4. _____ to do business

5. _____ to communicate with friends and family

6. _____ for fun (to listen to music or watch movies)

◑ Reading 1

A. Read the text on your own.

Why Is English a Global Language?

Why do people around the world learn English? First, people learn English to **communicate** with others outside of their **country**. In some countries, many people learn English very well. This is common in countries where the **language** is not used outside of the country. For example, people in Sweden **speak** English very well. Few people outside  of Sweden speak Swedish. Swedish people learn English to communicate globally. Because English is the language of **many** countries, many people study it. Then they can communicate with others. They can do business around the world.

Another reason English is a **global** language is because of **technology**. At first, it was difficult to use non-Roman alphabets on the computer. English uses the Roman alphabet. It is easy to type. In addition, many businesses use English on their websites. Most online information and **ideas** are in English. Other people want to share their ideas. They want people from other countries to read their ideas. They want to tell the world about their businesses. They use English on their websites. Now there are more people in the world who speak English as a second language than as a first language. Communication, business, and technology have all made English a global language.

B. Some words introduce ideas. Pause to say these words. They are important. They help you understand. Read the text again. Stress the words below.

First   *For example*   *Another reason*   *In addition*

Check Your Understanding

C. Circle the correct answer.

1. People learn English to communicate with people   *in* (*not in*) their country.

2. *Few*   *Many*   people speak Swedish outside of Sweden.

3. *Few*   *Many*   people use English to do business.

4. English   *is*   *is not*   easy to type on a keyboard.

5. *Many*   *Few*   people use English on their websites.

6. *Many*   *Few*   people speak English as a second language.

Vocabulary Strategy

Use a Dictionary

Sometimes you do not know the meaning of a word that is important in the text. You need to use a dictionary. A dictionary shows the word, the pronunciation, the part of speech, the meanings, and example sentences. The dictionary lists words in the order of the alphabet. Find the word *business* in the dictionary.

1. Start with the first letter. Find the *b* words.

2. Find the *bu* words.

3. Find the *bus* words.

bush·el /ˈbʊʃl/ *noun* [*count*]
a unit for measuring grain and fruit, equal to 64 pints or 35.2 liters: *a bushel of apples*

busi·ness 🔎 /ˈbɪznəs/ *noun* (*plural* **busi·ness·es**)
1 [*noncount*] buying and selling things: *I want to go into business when I leave school.* ◆ *Business is not very good this year.*
2 [*noncount*] the work that you do as your job: *The manager will be away on business next week.* ◆ *a business trip*
3 [*count*] a place where people sell or make things, for example a store or factory
it's none of your business; **mind your own business** words that you use to tell someone rudely that you do not want to tell them about something private: *"Where are you going?" "Mind your own business!"*

busi·ness·man /ˈbɪznəsˌmæn; ˈbɪznəsˌmən/ *noun* [*count*] (*plural* **busi·ness·men** /ˈbɪznəsˌmən/)
a man who works in business, especially in a top position

from *Oxford Basic American Dictionary*, ©Oxford University Press, 2011

GO ONLINE for more practice

D. Look at the dictionary entry for *business* in the Vocabulary Strategy box. Answer the questions.

1. What part of speech is *business*?

   a. noun   b. verb   c. adjective

2. Which meaning matches the meaning of *business* in the first paragraph of the text on page 74?

   a. 1   b. 2   c. 3

3. What word comes before *business* in the dictionary? _____

4. What word comes after *business* in the dictionary? _____

5. What is the plural form of *business*?

   a. businesses   b. /ˈbɪznəs/   c. business's

6. What type of noun is *business* in this sentence? *Many businesses use English on their websites.*

   a. count   b. noncount

E. Write the words in the order you would see them in the dictionary.

1. website	wonderful	wind	*website, wind, wonderful*
2. another	announce	ago	_____
3. carefully	careless	care	_____
4. direction	dinner	dollar	_____
5. grade	goods	govern	_____

Reading Strategy

Summarize

You summarize a text to tell the main idea. A summary includes only the most important information. Use these strategies:

1. Cross out sentences and phrases that add details.

2. Rewrite the important information in your own words.

> ~~Why do people around the world learn English?~~ First, people learn English to communicate with others outside of their country. ~~In some countries many people learn English very well. This is common in countries where the language is not used outside of the country. For example, people in Sweden speak English very well. Few people outside of Sweden speak Swedish. Swedish people learn English to communicate globally.~~ Because English is the language of many countries, many people study it. ~~Then they can communicate with others.~~ They can do business around the world.

Summary statement: *People learn English to communicate and do business.*

GO ONLINE
for more
practice

F. Cross out the sentences that are details. Then write a summary statement on the line below.

Another reason English is a global language is because of technology. At first, it was difficult to use non-Roman alphabets on the computer. English uses the Roman alphabet. It is easy to type. In addition, many businesses use English on their websites. Most online information and ideas are in English. Other people want to share their ideas. They want people from other countries to read their ideas. They want to tell the world about their businesses. Now there are more people in the world who speak English as a second language than as a first language. Communication, business, and technology have all made English a global language.

_____

◉ Reading 2

A. The text below has numbers. Some of the numbers are written as words, like *ninety*. Some of the numbers are written as numbers, like *260*.

1. Look at how we say these numbers.

   1400s = fourteen hundreds   15,000 = fifteen thousand   260 = two hundred sixty

2. Find the numbers in the text.

3. Practice reading them.

B. Now read the text on your own.

Why Do Languages Die?

In the 1400s, people around the world spoke about 15,000 **languages**. Now there are 7,000 languages. Every two weeks a language dies. Why do languages **die**? There are very few speakers of some languages. Sometimes young people stop **speaking** the language of their parents. They want to **communicate** with others. They learn other languages to communicate with **many** people around the world. In addition, they learn other languages so they can get jobs. Another reason is sometimes speakers of a language die. Then fewer people speak the language. There are

People make videos of speakers of different languages. Then the languages are not lost. People can listen and learn.

Stop and Think
What happens when a language dies?

no people left to teach it to others. When no one speaks a language, the language dies. It dies with the last speakers of the language.

Every **country** loses languages. Australia has 250 native languages. Ninety percent of these languages do not have many speakers. Canada and the United States have 260 native languages. Eighty percent are not being learned by young people. There are people who work to keep languages alive. They help people learn them. They make videos of the speakers. They don't want languages to die. Languages have words and phrases with information. Only the speakers know this information. This information is lost when the language dies. More and more people learn **global** languages like English. When fewer people learn a language, it is in danger. It can die.

Grammar in the Readings

Notice count and noncount nouns in the readings.

Some nouns are count. You can tell how many there are.

*There are 260 native **languages** in Australia.*

Other nouns are noncount. You cannot tell how many.

*Most online **information** is in English.*

Notice *a/an* + singular count nouns in the readings.

Use *a* with singular count nouns that begin with a consonant sound: *a **c**ountry*

Use *an* with singular count nouns that begin with a vowel sound: *an **i**dea*

GO ONLINE
for grammar practice

Check Your Understanding

C. Check the reasons languages die.

1. ___✓___ Young people stop speaking the language of their parents.

2. _____ People want to communicate with others.

3. _____ People learn other languages to get jobs.

4. _____ Speakers of a language die.

5. _____ People make videos of the speakers.

Recycle

the Vocabulary Strategy

Vocabulary Strategy: Use a Dictionary

D. Write a short answer to each question.

1. Is the word *alive* important to the text?

_____

2. What part of speech is *alive*?

_____

> **a·live** 🔊 /əˈlaɪv/ *adjective*
> living; not dead: *Are your grandparents alive?*
> **all¹** 🔊 /ɔl/ *adjective, pronoun*
> **1** every part of something; the whole of something: *She ate all the bread.* ◆ *It rained all day.*

from *Oxford Basic American Dictionary*, ©Oxford University Press, 2011

3. What is the meaning of *alive*? _____

4. What is the example sentence shown for *alive*? _____

E. Find a word in the text on page 77 that you do not know. Answer the questions about the word with a partner.

1. Use a dictionary. What is the word's part of speech? _____

2. What is the word's meaning? _____

3. What word comes before it in the dictionary? _____

4. What is the example sentence given for the word? _____

Reading Strategy: Summarize

F. Cross out the sentences that are details. Then write a summary statement on the line below.

> Every country loses languages. Ninety percent of Australia's 250 native languages do not have many speakers. Canada and the United States have 260 native languages. Eighty percent are not being learned by young people. There are people who work to keep languages alive. They help people learn them. They make videos of the speakers. They don't want languages to die. Languages have words and phrases with information. Only the speakers know this information. This information is lost when the language dies. More and more people learn global languages, like English. When fewer people learn a language, it is in danger. It can die.

_____

⬤ Make Connections: Text to Text

_____

A. Both texts answer a *why* question. Write the reasons that the writer gives for each.

1. Why is English a global language?

   a. _____

   b. _____

   c. _____

   d. _____

2. Why do languages die?

   a. _____

   b. _____

   c. _____

   d. _____

B. Look at both texts. Answer the questions for each text.

Questions	"Why Is English a Global Language?"	"Why Do Languages Die?"
1. Who communicates?		
2. What countries are talked about?		
3. What languages are talked about?		
4. What is the main idea?		

Summarizing and Retelling

A. Complete the sentences with the words from the box. Some of the words have to be changed to fit the sentences. For example, *idea* has to be changed to *ideas*. Then read the sentences to a partner to retell the ideas.

Adjectives	Nouns	Verbs
few	country	communicate
global	idea	die
many	language	speak
	technology	

1. In a(n) _____ world, people learn English to _____ with others.

2. People in different countries learn English so they can _____ to others outside their _____.

3. They use _____ to share their _____ and do business.

4. _____ people learn English. Sometimes young people don't learn the language of their families. Then there are _____ speakers left.

5. When there are no more speakers of a language, the language _____.

6. When a(n) _____ dies, information is lost.

B. Compare the two readings. On the left, write words from Reading 1. On the right, write words from Reading 2. Write words from both readings in the middle.

Word Partners

alternative idea

great idea

have an idea

welcome ideas

GO ONLINE
to practice
word partners ▶◀▲

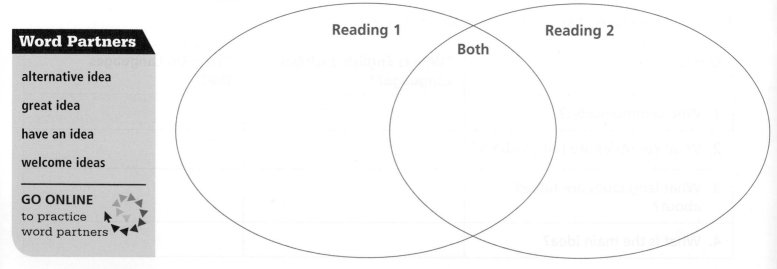

Reading 1   Both   Reading 2

● **Make Connections:** Text to World

A. Complete the chart with your own ideas.

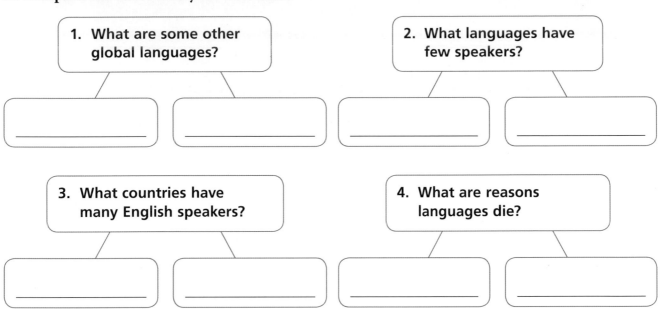

1. What are some other global languages?

2. What languages have few speakers?

3. What countries have many English speakers?

4. What are reasons languages die?

B. Think about the two texts. Complete the chart by making predictions.

Now	In the Year 2050 (future)
1. People use English to do business.	1. People will use _____.
2. People use English online and with technology.	2. People will use _____.
3. People learn English.	3. People will learn _____.
4. There are 7,000 languages.	4. There will be _____.

C. Complete each sentence with a word from the box.

because	important	in addition	summarize

1. Writers use the words _____ to add another idea.

2. Writers use the word _____ to explain why and give a reason.

3. Readers use a dictionary when they don't know the word and it is _____ to the text.

4. To _____, readers cross out the details and use their own words to tell the main ideas.

Chant

GO ONLINE
for the
Chapter 5
Vocabulary &
Grammar Chant

Why Do We Go on Vacation?

- Long o /oʊ/ and short i /ɪ/ sounds
- Comparative and superlative adjectives
- Visualize
- *does not* and *do not* + verbs; *always, often, never* with verbs

▲ BEFORE READING ► Oxford 2000 🔑 words to talk about vacations

Learn Vocabulary

A. Match each picture to the correct sentence.

_____ I like to study in a **quiet** place.

_____ I **prefer** riding my bike.

_____ I like to sit and **relax** in the park.

_____ I like to **visit** new cities.

_____ Rome is a **popular** city. Many people travel there.

__1__ I think sailing is **exciting**.

1.

2.

3.

4.

5.

6.

B. Match each picture to the correct sentence.

_____ I **plan** to visit Paris in May.   _____ We like **vacations** at the beach.

___1___ Mike went surfing. It was a big **adventure**!   _____ I go to my **local** market every day.

1.

2.

3.

4.

C. Answer the questions. You can circle more than one answer.

1. How do you **relax**?

   a. read   b. listen to music   c. sit in the sun

2. What do you think is **exciting**?

   a. meeting someone new   b. playing sports   c. watching a movie

3. When do you want to be in a **quiet** place?

   a. to sleep   b. to read   c. to talk to a good friend

4. What do you **prefer** to drink?

   a. coffee   b. tea   c. water

5. Where do you want to go for **vacation**?

   a. beach   b. city   c. mountains

6. What do you **plan** for?

   a. a vacation   b. the weekend   c. work

D. Answer the questions with a partner.

1. What are the **local** foods in your city?

2. What is a **popular** city people visit in your country?

Oxford 2000 🔑

Use the Oxford 2000 list on page 133 to find more words to describe the pictures on these pages. Share your words with a partner.

GO ONLINE for more practice

Preview the Text

E. Look at the pictures and text on page 86. Answer the questions.

1. Describe the pictures on page 86.

    a. Photo 1: _____

    b. Photo 2: _____

2. Read the first sentence below. Circle the noun the writer will talk about.

    You visit a city to see art, music, theater, and restaurants.

3. What do you think is the topic of the text?

    a. vacation in a city   b. exciting vacation places   c. relaxing on a beach

4. Who do you think the writer wrote the text for?

    a. local people   b. people on vacation   c. children

5. These words are in the text on page 86. Circle the word that does not have the same meaning. Use a dictionary for help.

    a. exciting   b. calm   c. quiet

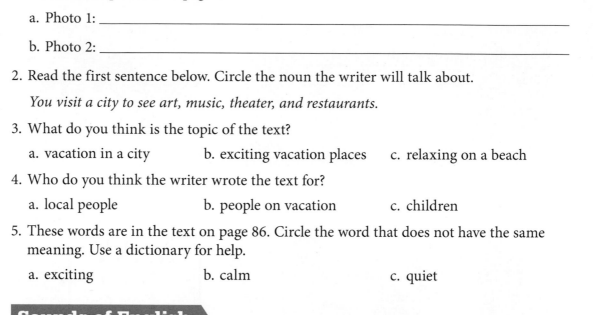

Sounds of English

Spelling Connection

🔊 A. Listen to the word *go*. What sound does the *o* make? Circle three words below that have the same sound as in *go*. Listen for /oʊ/. The letters *ow* sometimes make the sound in *go*. Other times they make the sound in *now*.

    cow   role   slow   do   low

B. Circle the vocabulary word that has the same sound as in *go*.

    adventure   exciting   local   popular

🔊 C. Listen to the word *sit*. What sound does the *i* make? Circle two words below that have the same sound as in *sit*. Listen for /ɪ/. The letter *e* sometimes makes the sound.

    sea   sick   silly   bed   reply

● Make Connections: Text to Self

A. Write a short answer to each question.

1. Where do people go on vacation in your country? _____

2. What do local people prefer to do in your city? _____

3. Where do you go on vacation? _____

4. Why do you go on vacation? _____

5. What is a popular city in the world to visit? _____

   Why? _____

6. How do you feel after a vacation? _____

B. Think about vacations in the city. Complete the web.

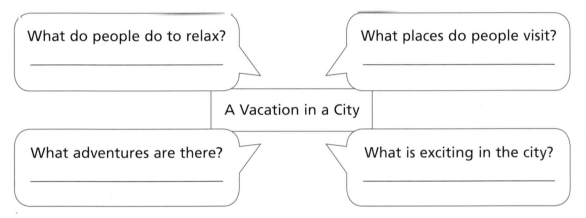

What do people do to relax?
_____

What places do people visit?
_____

A Vacation in a City

What adventures are there?
_____

What is exciting in the city?
_____

C. Write the phrases in the chart. Use a dictionary for help.

walk around a new city	sit in a park	buy clothes
meet new people	visit a popular place	look at art
eat local food	rest on a beach	see a theater show

I think these are exciting.	I think these are relaxing.

◉ Reading 1

A. Read the text on your own.

Finding Excitement and Calm in the City

You **visit** a city to see art, music, theater, and restaurants. You want to do new things. A **vacation** in a big city is always **exciting**. In 2013, Bangkok, Thailand, was the most **popular** city in the world. More international tourists visited there. Bangkok offers many **adventures**. You can visit the biggest market in the world. You can buy fresh mangoes, clothing, and furniture. Look at the sights in Chatuchak Market with the other 200,000 visitors. Walk along and see the bright colors of snakes, birds, and flowers. Then take a river boat to Patravadi Theatre. Watch the best dancers in Thailand.

The city streets are exciting, but people go on vacation to **relax**. After a relaxing vacation, people feel calmer. They share this calm feeling with others, and they feel relaxed, too. So, after you visit the market in Bangkok, find somewhere quieter. Follow the **local** people to beautiful Lumphini Park. Relax in the afternoon sun. Don't think about home for a few moments. Think of everything you saw. Enjoy this **quiet** place. You can relax in a busy city.

Buy fresh fruit at Chatuchak Market.

Relax in beautiful Lumphini Park.

B. Writers create a rhythm with their sentences. The sentences below all begin with verbs. The subject is *you*. Stress the verbs as you read. Notice the rhythm.

Follow the local people to beautiful Lumphini Park. Relax in the afternoon sun. Don't think about home for a few moments. Think of everything you saw. Enjoy this quiet place.

Check Your Understanding

C. Circle the correct answer.

1. The writer thinks you can relax in Bangkok.   (Yes)   No
2. The writer thinks it is best to do something exciting.   Yes   No
3. Cities have many adventures.   Yes   No
4. You have to take a boat to Lumphini Park.   Yes   No
5. People share their feelings of excitement with others.   Yes   No

Vocabulary Strategy

Comparative and Superlative Adjectives

When you compare, you tell about the differences between two things. Use comparative adjectives to compare.

     adjective   comparative

Paris is **nice**. *I think Buenos Aires is* **nicer**.

You can compare three things. Look at the different words.

     adjective   comparative   superlative

Paris is **nice**. *I think Buenos Aires is* **nicer**. *But Tokyo is* **the nicest**.

To make a comparative or superlative adjective, add the correct ending. Adjectives with one or two syllables use *-er* and *-est*. Adjectives with three or more syllables use *more* and *most*.

Adjective	Comparative	Superlative
nice	nicer	the nicest
exciting	more exciting	the most exciting

Some words don't follow these rules: *good/better/best*   *bad/worse/worst*

GO ONLINE
for more
practice

D. Complete the chart.

Adjective	Comparative	Superlative
1. big	bigger	_____
2. _____	_____	calmest
3. good	better	_____
4. popular	more popular	_____

Visualize

When you visualize, you read the words and create a picture in your head. Visualizing brings reading to life and makes the text easier to understand. Think of what you see, smell, and hear.

You can visit the biggest market in the world.

What does the market look like? Read more.

You can buy fresh mangoes, clothing, and furniture. Look at the sights in Chatuchak Market with the other 200,000 visitors. Walk along and see the bright colors of snakes, birds, and flowers.

Picture a big market with 200,000 people. The people are buying clothes, food, flowers, and pets. What colors do you see? What food is there? What does it smell like? What do you hear? Look at the picture and think of yourself in the market.

Look for sentences in the text that help you visualize. Sometimes these sentences begin with verbs. They help you visualize being in the place.

Follow the local people to beautiful Lumphini Park.

GO ONLINE
for more
practice

E. Read the sentences. Visualize to answer the questions.

Follow the local people to beautiful Lumphini Park. Relax in the afternoon sun. Don't think about home for a few moments. Think of everything you saw. Enjoy this quiet place.

1. How do you feel when you are in a park? _____

_____

2. What do you do in a park? _____

_____

3. What do you see and hear? _____

_____

4. Why are parks popular places? _____

_____

Then take a river boat to Patravadi Theatre. Watch the best dancers in Thailand.

5. How do you feel on a boat? _____

_____

6. What do you see at a theater? _____

_____

7. Why do people watch dancers? _____

_____

8. How does it feel to be in a theater? _____

◎ Reading 2

A. Preview the text. Then read it on your own.

Do Vacations Bring Happiness?

What is your favorite **vacation**? Is it skiing down a mountain? Do you **prefer** a beach? More and more people prefer an **exciting** vacation. They want an **adventure** to remember. They do not want to **relax**. They want the feeling of their heart beating fast. Climbing a mountain or surfing can feel great. Adventure vacations are **popular**. Any kind of vacation is good. A trip away from home and a **quiet** break from work often help people **relax**.

Does a vacation bring happiness? Actually, research shows that **planning** the vacation makes people happy. That is the most important part. Yes, that is right! Traveling can bring stress, but thinking about fun things to do brings happiness. **Visiting** somewhere new is always exciting. A vacation from work and school is fun. You don't have to answer the phone. You can turn off the computer. But people get real happiness from planning their vacation. People become happy by reading about their adventure. They visualize themselves in a new place. They don't think about everything at home. This is what brings happiness. Start thinking of different places. Read about every adventure. Sometimes the dream is better than the trip!

skiing in the Alps

surfing in the Pacific Ocean

Grammar in the Readings

Notice *does not* and *do not* + verbs in the readings.

Use *does/do not* + a verb to tell what is not true.

singular

⌐¬
He **does not** like skiing.

plural

⌐¬
They **do not** want to relax.

Notice *always, often, never* with verbs in the reading.

Use *always, often,* and *never* with verbs to tell how many times.

*Visiting somewhere new is **always** exciting. (all the time)*

*A quiet break from work **often** helps people relax. (many times)*

*I **never** go on vacation. (not at any time)*

Stop and Think

How do you feel on an adventure?

GO ONLINE
for grammar
practice

Check Your Understanding

B. Circle the correct answer.

1. More and more people want _____ vacation.

   a. a quiet   b. a popular   c. an adventure

2. _____ vacations are good for people.

   a. All   b. No   c. Adventure

3. New research shows _____.

   a. vacations help people relax   b. planning a vacation is fun   c. adventure vacations are the best

4. People get happiness from _____.

   a. planning and thinking   b. going on vacation   c. having an adventure

5. The main idea is _____.

   a. take a vacation   b. plan a vacation   c. have fun

Recycle

the Vocabulary Strategy

Vocabulary Strategy: Comparative and Superlative Adjectives

C. Complete the chart.

Adjective	Comparative	Superlative
1. _____	quieter	quietest
2. bad	_____	worst
3. important	more important	_____

D. Complete each sentence with a word from the chart in Activity C.

1. The food in Tokyo is _____ than the food at home.

2. My hotel is a(n) _____ place to relax than yours.

3. It is fun to go on vacation, but the _____ part is when it ends.

4. It is _____ to plan your trip before you go.

5. The park is relaxing. It's a(n) _____ place to visit.

Reading Strategy: Visualize

E. Read the sentences. Visualize to answer the questions.

More and more people prefer an exciting vacation. They want an adventure to remember. They want the feeling of their heart beating fast.

1. The writer says people prefer an exciting vacation. How does it feel to have your heart beat fast? _____

2. Look at the picture of people skiing on page 89. Think of yourself on the mountain. How do you feel? _____

3. Why is skiing exciting? _____

4. Climbing a mountain or surfing can feel great. Adventure vacations are popular. Look at the picture of surfing on page 89. Think of yourself in the water. How do you feel?

_____

⬤ **Make Connections: Text to Text**

A. Some of the sentences in both texts begin with verbs where the subject is *you*. The writer talks to you. Write sentences like the example in the chart.

"Finding Excitement and Calm in the City"	"Do Vacations Bring Happiness?"
Look at the sights in Chatuchak Market with the other 200,000 visitors.	

B. Both writers use words and phrases connected to the words *exciting* and *relaxing*. Write words and phrases from both texts in the chart.

Exciting	Relaxing

Summarizing and Retelling

A. Complete the sentences with the words from the box. Then read the paragraphs to a partner to summarize.

Adjectives	Nouns	Verbs
exciting	adventure	plan
local	vacation	prefer
popular		relax
quiet		visit

1.   Many people go on _____. It is fun to _____ a new place. Some people _____ a city vacation. They can walk the city streets and try the _____ food. It's exciting in a(n) _____ city, but people also want to relax. You can find _____ places in cities.

2.   An adventure is something you do that is _____. People like adventure vacations. Others prefer a place to _____. A(n) _____ is fun. But people get happiness when they _____ the vacation.

B. Match the answers to the questions.

1. _____ Why do people visit a city?

2. _____ Why do people go on vacation?

3. _____ What makes people happy?

4. _____ What happens when you relax on vacation?

5. _____ What kind of vacations are popular?

a. planning a vacation

b. to relax

c. to see art, music, theater, and restaurants

d. others feel relaxed

e. adventure vacations

Word Partners

be quiet

keep quiet

stay quiet

GO ONLINE
to practice
word partners

⬤ Make Connections: Text to World

A. Do you agree with the writers? Check the statements you agree with.

1. _____ People want an adventure on vacation.

2. _____ People want to visit local places on vacation.

3. _____ People feel relaxed because others are calm.

4. _____ People like to relax on vacation.

5. _____ Planning a vacation is fun.

6. _____ Planning a vacation is more fun than the trip.

B. Discuss your answers from Activity A with a partner.

C. What characteristics make something an adventure? Look at the Oxford 2000 keywords on page 133 and find five words to help you. Complete the web.

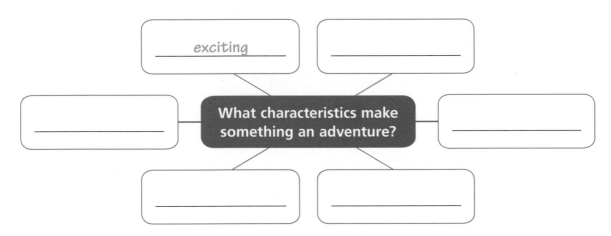

D. Think about texts that describe vacations. What makes the text good?

1. The writer talks about _____

2. The writer uses _____

3. The text is _____

E. Did the writers do a good job? Check the things each writer did well.

	Reading 1	Reading 2
1. describe places and help the reader visualize	_____	_____
2. show pictures to support the ideas	_____	_____
3. use research and facts for supporting main ideas	_____	_____
4. begin sentences with verbs and talk to the reader	_____	_____
5. use examples to support the main idea	_____	_____

Chant

GO ONLINE
for the
Chapter 6
Vocabulary &
Grammar Chant

Look at the word bank for Unit 2. Check (✓) the words you know.
Circle the words you want to learn better.

OXFORD 2000 🔑

Adjectives	Nouns		Verbs
exciting	adventure	planet	communicate
few	country	size	die
global	distance	technology	explore
local	idea	vacation	plan
many	land		prefer
popular	language		relax
quiet	map		speak
	ocean		visit

PRACTICE WITH THE OXFORD 2000 🔑

A. Use the words in the chart. Match adjectives with nouns.

1. _____popular idea_____   2. _____

3. _____   4. _____

5. _____

B. Use the words in the chart. Match verbs with nouns.

1. _____explore land_____   2. _____

3. _____   4. _____

5. _____

C. Use the words in the chart. Match verbs with adjective noun partners.

1. _prefer exciting adventure_   2. _____

3. _____   4. _____

5. _____

UNIT 3 Things

UNIT WRAP UP ## Extend Your Skills

CHAPTER 7

What Inventions Changed the World?

- Long i /ɑɪ/ sound
- Word families
- Signal words for time
- Simple past; *was* and *were*

▲ BEFORE READING ► Oxford 2000 ✎ words to talk about inventions

Learn Vocabulary

A. Match each picture to the correct sentence.

_____ You use a **camera** to take photographs.

_____ Birds and planes **fly**.

_____ The **past** is the time before now. It is part of history.

_____ When you **imagine** something, you create a picture of it in your head.

_____ **Speed** is how fast something goes.

_1_ When you **invent** something, you create something new.

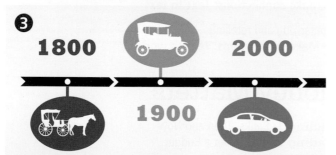

B. Complete each sentence with a word from the box.

~~now~~	develop	possible	then

1. We use _____ now _____ to talk about things that happen at this time.

2. We use _____ to talk about things that happened before. They are in the past.

3. When something is _____, you can do it.

4. When you _____ something, you make it. You create it.

C. Look at the pictures. Complete the paragraphs with the words from the box.

camera	fly	invent	past	speeds
develop	~~imagine~~	now	possible	then

1.   Can you _____ imagine _____ the world to be a different place? In 1903, the Wright brothers did. They were the first inventors to build a plane and safely _____ it. Planes move at high _____. They are faster than cars and trains.

    To _____ something, you have to imagine. You think of what is _____. Then you _____ it. The Wright brothers created a plane.

Oxford 2000 🔑

Use the Oxford 2000 list on page 133 to find more words to describe the pictures on these pages. Share your words with a partner.

2.   Now everyone has a _____. But in the _____, cameras were not common. _____ they were not small. You couldn't take pictures easily. _____ cameras are much smaller. Most phones have cameras on them.

D. Answer the questions with a partner.

1. Imagine the world better than it is now. Describe it.

2. What do you want someone to invent?

GO ONLINE for more practice

Preview the Text

E. Look at the pictures on page 100. Match the answers to the questions.

1. Who are the men in the photo on the right? _____   a. a steamship

2. What did they invent? _____   b. the Wright brothers

3. What does the photo on the left show? _____   c. travel

4. Both photos show different ways to _____ .   d. a plane

F. Write a short answer to each question.

1. What is the topic of the text? _____

_____

2. What years does the first paragraph talk about? _____

3. What years does the second paragraph talk about? _____

Sounds of English

Spelling Connection

A. Listen to the word *five*. What sound does the *i* make? Circle three words below that have the same sound as in *five*. Listen for /aɪ/. The letter *y* sometimes makes the sound in *five*.

bite   analyze   complain   with   combine

B. Circle the vocabulary word that has the same sound as in *five*.

camera   fly   imagine   invent   possible

C. These words are in the text on page 100. Circle two words with the long i sound as in *five*.

trip   flight   it   sail   time   million

● Make Connections: Text to Self

A. Answer the questions.

1. Why did people invent the airplane? _____

2. How did we travel before the airplane? _____

3. What speed do planes travel at? _____

4. What speed do cars go? _____

5. List four ways to travel. _____

_____

_____

B. What do you know about planes? How do they work? What makes them safe? Use the words from the box to tell what you know about plane travel. Use a dictionary for help.

air	distance	land	map	safe	speed	time

1. _____

2. _____

3. _____

4. _____

C. Complete the web.

We can explore our world and visit new places.

How have planes changed our world?
What can we do now?

◉ Reading 1

A. Read the text on your own.

The Way We Travel

Stop and Think

How do you feel on an adventure? What does *before then* mean? Read the sentences before these words again.

In the 1900s, the steam train went 125 miles per hour. The **speed** of travel was about to change. Before **then**, people **imagined** flying. In the **past**, they **invented** flying machines. But the machines were not successful. The flight by the Wright brothers on December 17, 1903, was a success. It did three important things. First, the plane lifted into the air on its own. Second, the plane moved forward and did not lose **speed**. Third, it landed at the same height it started at. **Now**, plane travel was **possible**. For the first time, it was safe to **fly**.

In the 1500s, explorers from England sailed across the Atlantic in 92 days. In 1838, a steamship did it in about 15 days. Now, you can make the same trip from England to America in a six-hour flight. Plane travel changed our world. Today, we can go anywhere in one day. We often travel for fun and for work. We travel to explore. In 1903, we had flight, and in 1969, we landed on the moon. Now each day about eight million people fly all over the world. Flight changed the speed of travel. It changed the time of travel. It changed our understanding of the world.

In the 1800s, a steamship traveled for 15 days across the Atlantic.

The Wright brothers' plane in 1903.

B. Reading sentences or parts of sentences again can help you understand. What does *about to change* mean? The writer is talking about the speed of a steam train. *About to change* means the speed of travel is going to change.

C. Stop and read the text again to help you understand.

Check Your Understanding

D. Circle the correct answer.

1. The Wright brothers were the first to invent a flying machine.   (Yes)   No

2. Planes travel at 125 miles per hour.   Yes   No

3. One of the reasons the flight was successful is that it did not lose speed.   Yes   No

4. Explorers sailed the Atlantic before steamships.   Yes   No

5. In the past, explorers sailed for 92 days to cross the Atlantic.   Yes   No

6. Eight million people fly each hour of the day.   Yes   No

Vocabulary Strategy

Word Families

Some words are in the same family. The parts of speech are different. The meanings are similar. If you understand what part of speech a word is, it will help you understand the word better.

     noun   verb

The flight was a **success**. *It was able to* **succeed** *for three reasons.*

       adjective

Earlier machines were not **successful**.

Nouns name people, places, or things. They often have the word *the*, *a*, or *an* before them. Verbs describe actions. Verbs sometimes have the word *to* before them. Adjectives describe a noun.

Noun	Verb	Adjective
flight	fly	
invention/inventor*	invent	
imagination	imagine	
success	succeed	successful

* *The ending* -or *on* inventor, director, *and other words is for a person. An inventor is someone who invents.*

GO ONLINE
for more
practice

E. Complete each sentence with a word from the chart in the Vocabulary Strategy box.

1. Before the _____ of the steamship, people sailed across the ocean.

2. You need a good _____ to invent something.

3. I want to be an _____. I have a good imagination, and I like to create things.

4. My family members work hard. They _____ in life.

Signal Words for Time

Signal words for time help you answer the question *When?*

Sometimes the signal is a year or date.

> **In the 1900s,** *the steam train went 125 miles per hour.*

Sometimes the signal is a word or phrase.

> *Before* **then,** *people imagined flying.*

What does *then* refer to? You have to look back at the text. *Then* refers to the 1900s.

> **Now,** *plane travel was possible.*

What does *now* refer to? Look back at the text. *Now* refers to 1903 when the Wright brothers flew their plane.

GO ONLINE
for more
practice

F. Read the sentences. Write the missing time signal.

1. The flight by the Wright brothers on ___December 17, 1903___, was a success.

2. _____, explorers from England sailed across the Atlantic in 92 days.

3. _____, a steamship did it in about 15 days.

4. _____, we can go anywhere in one day.

5. _____, we had flight and _____, we landed on the moon.

G. Write short answers to show the events on the timeline.

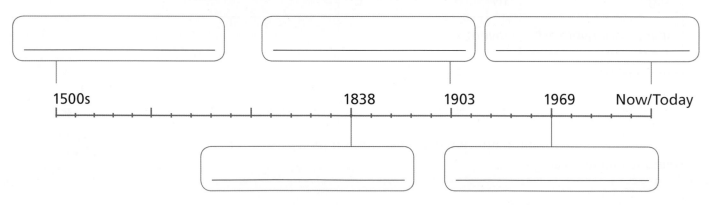

◄)) Reading 2

A. Preview the text. Then read it to yourself.

It's in a Picture

What was the last picture you took? Was it a picture of you? What were you doing? Pictures show our lives. They are a way to say: "I was here. I did this. Look at me." Pictures tell our stories. We share pictures with our friends and family. We take pictures of the food we eat, the places we go, and the people we see. Today, people remember things from their pictures. Often, we see our pictures, and we think of the **past**. These pictures become our memories. **Cameras** tell our stories.

In the 1820s, Joseph Nicéphore Niépce wanted to **develop** a way to take pictures. He had some success. But the pictures didn't last. You saw them one day but not the next. The picture didn't stay. **Then** in 1826 or

This is the first photograph of a person, taken by Louis Daguerre in 1838.

1827, he took a picture from the window of his house in France. It showed his buildings and land. It was the first photograph. You can see the picture today. Then in 1838, Louis Daguerre took the first photograph of a person. In this picture, there is a man. He is not moving because he is getting his boots shined. The Paris streets look empty because all the other people were moving. The picture does not show them. Daguerre needed several minutes to take one picture. **Now**, it's **possible** to see our pictures in less than a second. In a picture, we stop time. We make the moment last.

Grammar in the Readings

Notice the simple past in the readings.

Writers use the simple past to talk about things in the past. Many verbs in the simple past end in -*ed*.

*The plane **landed**.*   *Plane travel **changed** our world.*

Notice *was* and *were* in the readings.

Writers also use *was* and *were* to talk about things in the past. You can use *was* with a singular subject and *were* with a plural subject.

singular
$\vert$
*I **was** here.*

plural
$\vert$
*The Wright brothers **were** inventors.*

Stop and Think

Do you agree with the writer? Why do you take pictures?

GO ONLINE
for grammar
practice

Check Your Understanding

B. Match each part to make a sentence.

1. Pictures are a way to say I ___b___ .

2. Today, people _____ things from their pictures.

3. Niépce had some success, but the picture _____ .

4. Niépce took a picture from _____ .

a. remember

b. was here

c. the window of his house

d. didn't last

C. Read the first sentence. Circle the sentence that has the same meaning.

1. Pictures become our memories.

   a. When we imagine the past, we often see the pictures we took.

   b. People take pictures of things they think are interesting.

2. But the pictures didn't last. The picture didn't stay.

   a. It was not possible to see the picture. The camera did not work.

   b. The camera worked, but then the picture disappeared.

Recycle

the Vocabulary
Strategy

Vocabulary Strategy: Word Families

D. Complete the chart.

Noun	Verb	Adjective
development	_____	
possibility		_____
emptiness		_____

E. Complete the sentences with a word from the chart in Activity D.

1. No one was in the store. It was _____ .

2. It is _____ to take pictures underwater.

3. Inventors _____ new things. Often they try many things before they are successful.

Recycle

the Reading
Strategy

Reading Strategy: Signal Words for Time

F. Read the sentences. Number them in the correct order.

_____ Then in 1826 or 1827, he took a picture from the window of his house in France.

_____ Then in 1838, Louis Daguerre took the first photograph of a person.

_____ Now, it's possible to see our pictures in less than a second.

___1___ In the 1820s, Joseph Nicéphore Niépce was trying to develop a way to take pictures.

⬤ Make Connections: Text to Text

A. Both texts talk about developments in the past. Name the development and then list the effects. What is true today because of the development?

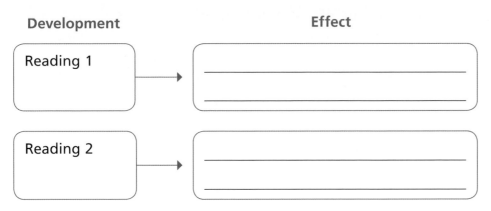

Development

Reading 1

Reading 2

Effect

B. Both texts name years and talk about what happened in those years. But the texts do not talk about the events in the order they happened. Why? Complete the paragraphs with the dates from the box.

| 1500s | 1826 or 1827 | 1838 | 1900s | 1903 | today | 1838 |

1. In Reading 1, the writer first talks about the _____ . People traveled by steam trains then. The writer then discusses a new development in _____ . The plane changed our world.

2. In Reading 1, in the second paragraph the writer talks about the _____ . In those years, explorers crossed the Atlantic. Then the writer discusses _____ . That was when a steamship took 15 days to cross the Atlantic. The writer ends by discussing how long it takes to fly _____ .

3. In Reading 2, the writer talks about photographs. The first paragraph is about why we take pictures. The second paragraph talks about the past. In _____ , Joseph Nicéphore Niépce took the first photograph. In _____ , Louis Daguerre took a photograph of a person. The text ends by talking about cameras now.

C. Answer the questions with a partner.

1. Why did the writer of Reading 1 talk about the events in that order?

2. Why did the writer of Reading 2 talk about the events in that order?

3. What do you think is the best order for the events in each reading?

▲▲▲ AFTER READING

Summarizing and Retelling

A. Complete the sentences with the words from the box. Some of the words have to be changed to fit the sentences. For example, *develop* has to be changed to *developed*. Then read the paragraphs to a partner to summarize.

Adjectives	Nouns	Verbs	Adverbs
possible	camera past speed	develop fly imagine invent	now then

1.   The texts are similar. Both texts tell about people. They _____ new inventions. Both writers use the word _____ to talk about events in the past. Both writers use the word _____ to talk about today. The inventors in the texts _____ the world differently. Their work changed our world.

2.   The texts are different. The first text talks about the _____ of travel. The Wright brothers _____ the first plane. Now, we can _____ anywhere. Flight made landing on the moon _____ . The second text talks about the development of the _____ . In the _____ , people did not see their pictures quickly. Now people see their pictures in less than a second. Everyone uses a camera.

B. Answer the questions.

1. The writer listed reasons why the Wright brothers' flight was successful. Write three reasons.

    a. First, _____

    b. Second, _____

    c. Third, _____

2. The writer listed reasons we take pictures. Write three reasons.

    a. _____

    b. _____

    c. _____

Word Partners

in the past

distant past

from your past

GO ONLINE
to practice
word partners

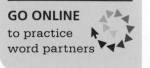

⬤ Make Connections: Text to World

A. Think about the two texts. Complete the web.

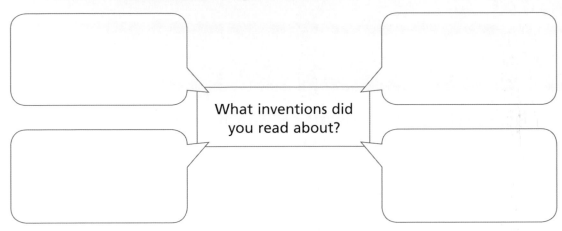

What inventions did you read about?

B. Check the reasons people read about inventions.

1. _____ to learn about the past

2. _____ to understand how something works

3. _____ to understand how the world was different

4. _____ to understand the order of events

5. _____ to compare today with the past

6. _____ to learn about the inventors

7. _____ to imagine the world differently

8. _____ to understand why something is successful

C. Compare your answers from Activity B with a partner. Then write another reason people read about inventions. What can we learn?

_____

D. Think about inventions you are interested in. Look at the Oxford 2000 keywords on page 133 and find five words to help you. Complete the web.

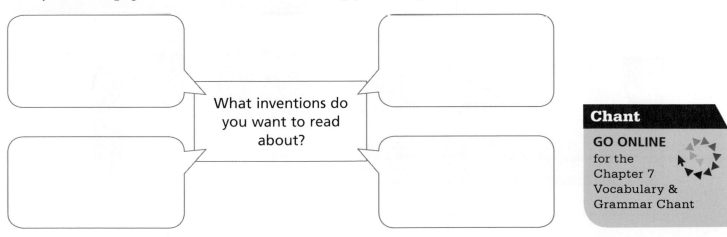

What inventions do you want to read about?

Chant

GO ONLINE for the Chapter 7 Vocabulary & Grammar Chant

Jobs and Skills in the 21st Century

- Schwa /ə/ and long e /i/
- Suffix *-er*
- Identify pronoun references
- *the* + nouns; verbs + *about*

▲ BEFORE READING ▶ Oxford 2000 🔑 words to talk about jobs

Learn Vocabulary

A. Write each sentence below the correct picture.

I **need** a coat!	I **design** cars.
I **work** with people. I help them feel better.	~~Research helps us learn more about sicknesses.~~

1.

Research helps us learn more about sicknesses.

2.

3.
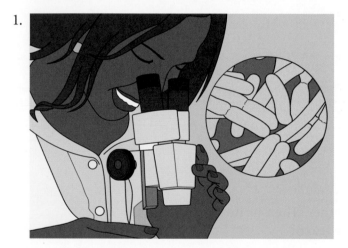

4.
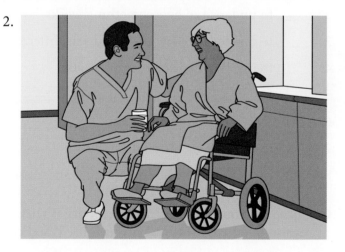

B. Match each picture to the correct description.

_____ I'm a server. My **job** is difficult.

__1__ I drive a truck. This is a special **skill**.

_____ I work in the computer **field**.

_____ I went to **medical** school. Now I am a doctor.

_____ I am the **manager** of a store.

_____ My **employer** is very nice.

C. Read the names of the fields and the jobs in the fields. Underline the jobs you know. Circle the ones you want to learn about.

Field	Jobs
medical	doctor, nurse, scientist, medical assistant
educational	teacher, writer, teacher's assistant
computer	technology designer, technology support assistant
financial	accountant, bank worker, office assistant
service	servers, cashiers, mechanics

Oxford 2000 🔑

Use the Oxford 2000 list on page 133 to find more words to describe the pictures on these pages. Share your words with a partner.

GO ONLINE
for more
practice

Preview the Text

D. Look at the picture and text on page 112. Answer the questions.

1. Write the name of three jobs you think are in the text. _____

_____

2. Write three fields you think the text will discuss. _____

_____

3. Look at the pictures. Why do you think the writer uses these pictures? _____

_____

4. Read the first sentence on page 112. The text describes _____ .

5. The words below are in the text. Use two of the words to write a sentence you think
   will be in the text.

   jobs   *field*   *design*   *manager*   *research*   *medical*

_____

Sounds of English

Spelling Connection

A. Listen to the word *about*. What sound does the *a* make in the first syllable?
This sound is called schwa /ə/. It is not stressed. The syllable with schwa does
not have a strong vowel sound.

Circle three words below that have a syllable with the same sound as in *about*.
Listen for /ə/. This sound can be made by any vowel.

beat   disagree   plate   ahead   camera

B. Circle the vocabulary words that have the same sound as in *about*.

design   field   manager   research

employer   job   need   work

C. Listen to the word *see*. What sound does the *ee* make? Circle three words
below that have the same sound as in *see*. Listen for /i/.

movie   belt   meet   meat   news

D. Circle the vocabulary words that have the same sound as in *see*.

design   field   manager   research

employer   job   need   work

E. These words are in the text on page 112. Circle the words with the schwa
sound /ə/ as in *about* and underline the words with the long e sound as in *see*.

addition   people   computer   different   technology

⬤ Make Connections: Text to Self

A. Complete the chart. Write the name of a person you know, the person's job, and the field the job is in. Some possible jobs are listed in the box.

teacher	medical assistant	cashier	server
doctor	accountant	scientist	technology designer
office assistant	bank worker	teacher's assistant	technology support assistant
nurse	mechanic	writer	

Name	Job	Field

1. Compare your chart with a partner's chart. What jobs are popular?

_____

2. Why do you think they are popular? _____

B. What is changing in the world now? What jobs are needed? Complete the chart.

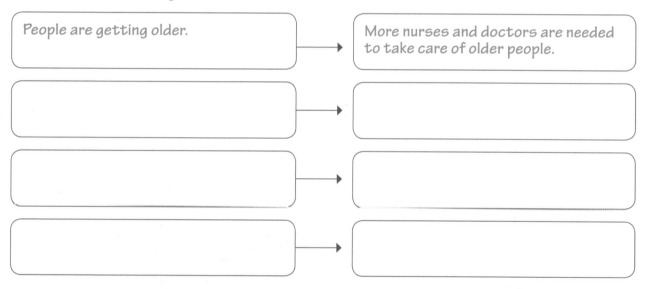

Change	Jobs Needed
People are getting older.	More nurses and doctors are needed to take care of older people.

C. Discuss your ideas from Activity B with a partner. Then list three skills you think the new jobs need.

_____   _____   _____

D. The writers talk about the jobs people do. Some people *do research*. Others *do medical work*. What kind of work do you do? _____

▲▲ DURING READING
▶ Vocabulary strategy: Suffix -*er*
▶ Reading strategy: Identify pronoun references

◉ Reading 1

A. Read the text on your own.

What Jobs Are We Going to Need?

Stop and Think

What skills and training do medical researchers need?

People have to **work**. They need **jobs**. What **fields** have jobs? Most important, what jobs will we **need** in the future? The medical field is going to need workers. In 2010, there were 524 million people over the age of 65 in the world. In 2050, the number of older people will be three times bigger. We need nurses and other **medical** workers to care for them. We also need family doctors. Family doctors have to work many hours. Because of this, not very many medical students study to be family doctors. They become other kinds of doctors, like heart doctors. In addition, there are jobs for medical researchers. They do **research** and develop new medicines and technology to help people. Businesses want to sell this medicine and technology to people who need it.

Medical researchers develop new medicine. The medicine helps sick people get better.

Another popular field is the computer field. It is a field with different kinds of jobs. Some people, like IT **managers**, help people in schools, hospitals, and companies when they have computer problems. Other people **design** and create new technology. For example, 20 percent of people in the world have a smartphone. This is a phone that can do the same things computers do. More and more people are using technology, so businesses are always designing newer computers and phones. What common characteristic do these jobs share? People need the help of these workers. This is why these fields are growing. If there is a need, there is a job.

B. Some words connect ideas. Look for these words: *in addition, another, and.* **Read the text again to understand the ideas.**

C. Other words introduce examples. Read the text again and look for examples. What ideas do the examples support?

Check Your Understanding

D. Complete the sentences with the words from the box.

family doctors	medical	computer	~~nurses~~
fields	money manager	IT manager	need

1. There are not enough _____*nurses*_____ and

_____ .

2. Two popular fields are the _____ and

_____ fields.

3. What job is not in the reading? _____

4. Who helps people in schools and businesses when they have computer problems?

_____

5. These _____ are growing because people

_____ the help of these workers.

Vocabulary Strategy

Suffix -*er*

Understanding suffixes helps you make new words. A suffix is an ending added to a base word. The suffix has meaning and shows the part of speech of the word. The suffix -*er* is added to verbs to change them to nouns. The new word is a person:
teach + -er = teacher

   verb   noun

I **teach** *small children. I am a* **teacher***.*

Some words like *write* and *manage* end in *e*. Add *r* to these words. These words describe people: *writer, manager*

Not all words that end in -*er* follow this rule. Some words are not about people: *bigger, computer*

GO ONLINE
for more
practice

E. Add the suffix -*er* to each word below. Fill in the blank to tell the meaning of the new word. Then write a skill you think each person needs.

1. design: A ___*designer*___ is someone who ___*designs*___ . Skill: ___*creativity*___

2. work: A _____ is someone who _____ . Skill: _____

3. research: A _____ is someone who _____ . Skill: _____

4. write: A _____ is someone who _____ . Skill: _____

5. manage: A _____ is someone who _____ . Skill: _____

6. employ: An _____ is someone who _____ . Skill: _____

F. What words from the text on page 112 have *-er* and mean "someone who"?

_____   _____   _____

GO ONLINE
for more
practice

Reading Strategy

Identify Pronoun References

Pronouns are words that refer to a noun. Writers use pronouns to talk about a noun. Understanding pronouns will help you know what the writer is talking about.

> <u>People</u> have to work. **They** need jobs

The writer uses *they* to refer to people. The writer uses the pronoun so she doesn't have to repeat the noun.

He refers to a singular male, *she* refers to a singular female, and *it* refers to a singular object or idea.

> <u>Mr. An</u> is an accountant. **He** works many hours.

They refers to more than one male, female, or object.

> Because of this, not very many <u>medical students</u> study to be family doctors. **They** become other kinds of doctors, like heart doctors.

G. Read the sentences. Write the word the pronoun refers to.

1. My favorite writer is Charlotte Bronte. <u>She</u> wrote *Jane Eyre*.

   <u>   Charlotte Bronte   </u>

2. My brother got a new job. <u>He</u> begins tomorrow. _____

3. My dad repairs cell phones. <u>They</u> are small and easy to break.

   _____

4. Many people are sick and need doctors. <u>They</u> need medical care.

   _____

5. The technology field is growing, and <u>it</u> pays well. _____

⦿ Reading 2

A. Look at the illustration. Read the first sentence of each paragraph. What will the writer discuss? Now read the text.

What Skills Do Businesses Want?

Employers want the right people for their company. What do employers usually look for? They want someone with **skills** in their field. Sometimes the skills you have are more important than where you **worked**. When you have the skills, you can learn any **job**. So what skills are important? Businesses need people with strong communication skills: writing and speaking. They need people who are friendly and work well with others. In addition,

In a job interview, the manager will ask many questions.

managers want workers who can solve problems. This means they want people to use their own ideas when there is a problem. This skill includes getting information and analyzing it. Managers in many different **fields** look for people with these skills.

However, employers also look for something else. They want to understand who you are. What kind of a person are you? In a job interview, they may ask questions to find out about your interests. For example, maybe you run races. This shows you are a hard worker. Or maybe you like to read. This shows you have interests and are probably a good writer. Employers want to see what you know about your field. And they want to know what makes you different from other people.

Grammar in the Readings

Notice *the* + nouns in the readings.

Use *the* + nouns to talk about a specific noun.

> ***The medical field** is going to need workers.*

Use *the* + nouns after you have talked about the noun.

> *Employers want someone with <u>skills</u>. Sometimes **the skills you have** are more important than where you worked.*

Some nouns always have *the* before them.

> *For example, 20 percent of people in **the world** have a smartphone.*

Notice verbs + *about* in the readings.

Some verbs are followed by *about*.

> *They want to see what you **know about** your field.*
> *What does the text **talk about**?*

Stop and Think

Do you think job interviews are difficult?

GO ONLINE
for grammar practice

Check Your Understanding

B. Circle the correct answer.

1. Employers want people with _____ .

   a. interests   (b.) skills   c. fields

2. The first skill the writer talks about is _____ .

   a. being nice   b. solving problems   c. communicating

3. Working well with others means _____ .

   a. analyzing   b. being friendly   c. being important

4. Managers want workers to _____ problems.

   a. solve   b. use   c. analyze

5. Managers in different _____ look for people with these skills.

   a. jobs   b. fields   c. interviews

Vocabulary Strategy: Suffix -*er*

Recycle

the Vocabulary Strategy

C. Answer each question with a word with the suffix -*er*.

1. What do you call someone who <u>reads</u>? _____ reader _____

2. What do you call someone who <u>employs</u> people? _____

3. What do you call someone who <u>interviews</u> people for jobs? _____

4. What do you call someone who <u>reports</u> the news? _____

D. Complete each sentence with a word from the box.

dancer	interviewer	reader	employer

1. My _____ owns a big business. The company employs about 600 people.

2. I am a _____ . I perform on stage. I practice dance for many hours each day.

3. The _____ asked me many questions. Some were very difficult to answer.

4. My little brother is five. He loves books. He is a great _____ .

Reading Strategy: Identify Pronoun References

Recycle

the Reading Strategy

E. Read the sentences. Circle the noun or phrase the underlined pronoun refers to.

1. What do (employers) usually look for? <u>They</u> want someone with skills in their field.

2. Businesses need people with strong communication skills: writing and speaking. <u>They</u> need people who are friendly and work well with others.

3. This skill includes getting information and analyzing <u>it</u>.

4. Employers want to see what you know about your field. And <u>they</u> want to know what makes you different from other people.

⬤ Make Connections: Text to Text

A. Both texts answer questions. Write the question from the title and the answers from the text.

Question   Answer

Reading 1 → _____
              _____

Reading 2 → _____
              _____

B. Both texts give reasons to support the answers to the questions they ask. Write a short answer to each question.

1. Why are nurses and doctors needed? _____

_____

2. Why are there jobs in the medical research field? _____

_____

3. Why are there jobs in the computer field? _____

_____

4. Why do managers ask people what their interests are? _____

_____

5. Why do managers want to know you have the right skills? _____

_____

C. Both writers use words to show the connection between ideas. Match each sentence to the sentence that comes after it.

1. In a job interview, they may ask questions to find out about your interests. __d__

2. They become other kinds of doctors, like heart doctors. _____

3. Businesses want to sell this medicine and technology to people who need it. _____

4. They need people who are friendly and work well with others. _____

5. Employers want to see what you know about your field. _____

6. Other people design and create new technology. _____

a. **For example**, 20 percent of people in the world have a smartphone.

b. **And** they want to know what makes you different from other people.

c. **Another** popular field is the computer field.

d. ~~**For example**, maybe you run races.~~

e. **In addition**, managers want workers who can solve problems.

f. **In addition**, there are jobs for medical researchers.

Summarizing and Retelling

A. Complete the paragraphs with the words from the box. Some of the words have to be changed to fit the sentences. For example, *employer* has to be changed to *employers*. Then read the paragraphs to a partner to retell the ideas.

Adjectives	Nouns	Verbs
medical	employer	design
	field	need
	jobs	work
	manager	
	research	
	skill	

1. Both writers discuss the 21st century. In the first text, the writer talks about

    _____ we are going to need. The _____ field is

    growing. Some people in this field do _____ to help others. There are

    also jobs in the computer _____ . These people

    _____ cell phones and small computers. People

    _____ the help of these workers.

2. The second text talks about _____ . _____ and

    _____ look for people with good communication skills. They want

    people who _____ well with others. The text talks about job

    interviews and questions managers ask. What skills do you have? What are your

    interests? Managers want to know what you know about your field.

B. Think about the two texts. Answer the questions.

1. Do the writers answer the question in the title? _____

2. Write a new title for each text. _____

_____

3. Which text was more interesting? _____

   Why? _____

Word Partners

new skills

good skills

poor skills

old skills

basic skills

special skills

GO ONLINE
to practice
word partners

● Make Connections: Text to World

A. Complete the web with your own ideas. Look at the Oxford 2000 keywords on page 133 and find three words to help you.

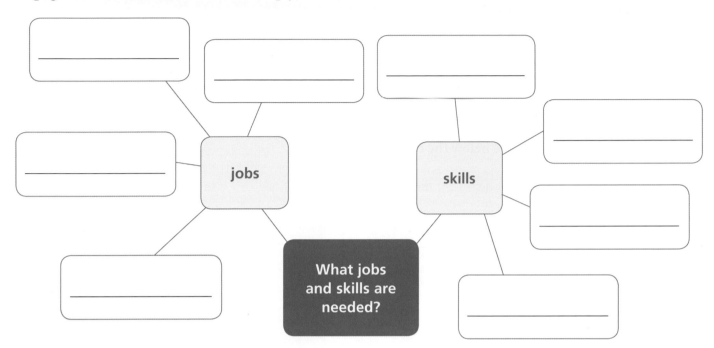

B. Compare your answers from Activity A with a partner. Answer the questions.

1. What are the most important skills?

2. Which jobs need those skills?

3. How do people learn those skills?

4. Why are the jobs needed?

5. What is the most interesting job?

C. Write a short answer to each question.

1. Where do people read about jobs? _____

2. Why do people read about jobs? _____

3. Where do people learn job skills? _____

4. What do employers want to find out about you? _____

Chant

GO ONLINE
for the
Chapter 8
Vocabulary &
Grammar Chant

- Long a /eɪ/ sound
- Financial collocations
- Analyze charts and spreadsheets
- *want to* + verbs; present progressive

▲ BEFORE READING ▶ Oxford 2000 🔑 words to talk about money

Learn Vocabulary

A. Write each word or phrase below the correct picture.

| **borrow** money | ~~money~~ | **spend** money | **save** money |

1.

money

2.

3.

4.

B. Match each picture to the correct vocabulary word.

_____ debt   _____ cost   _____ choice

_____ customer   _____ bank   __1__ pay

How much is this?

$75

C. Complete the paragraphs with the words from the box.

~~banks~~	borrow	costs	debt	pay

People use _____banks_____ . Sometimes they _____ money

from the bank so they can _____ for something that

_____ a lot, like a house. Then they are in _____ .

They have to pay back the money.

choices	customers	money	save	spend

It is difficult to _____ money, but most people find it easy to

_____ money. That is because _____ have so many

_____ . They can buy things online or in stores. If you have

_____ , you can get what you want.

Oxford 2000 🔑

Use the Oxford 2000 list on page 133 to find more words to describe the pictures on these pages. Share your words with a partner.

GO ONLINE
for more practice

Preview the Text

D. Look at the picture and text on page 124. Answer the questions.

1. The picture shows _____.

   a. information someone gives to a bank   b. information the bank gives to someone

2. The text will _____.

   a. describe the characteristics of someone   b. define and explain something

3. What question will the text answer?

   a. How do I get a bank account?   b. How are banks changing?

4. Read the first sentence of the text. Answer the question in the first sentence.

   _____

5. Read the description below the picture. What does the word *form* mean?

   a. a piece of paper   b. a shape

Sounds of English

Spelling Connection

🔊 A. Listen to the word *say*. What sound does the letter *a* make? Circle three words below that have the same sound as in *say*. Listen for /eɪ/.

    day   paid   animal   any   able

B. Circle the vocabulary words that have the same sound as in *say*.

    save   choice   borrow   customer   pay

C. These words are in the text on page 124. Circle three words with the long a sound as in *say*.

    have   human   safe   same   makes

● Make Connections: Text to Self

A. Complete the web. Use the bold words in the text on page 124 to help you.

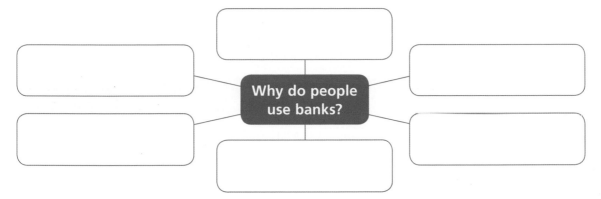

Why do people use banks?

B. What do people spend money on? What do people save money for? What do people borrow money for? List your ideas in the web.

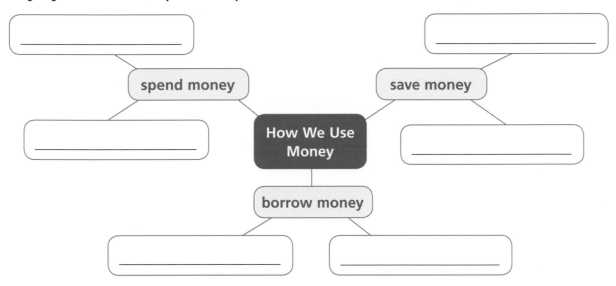

spend money

save money

How We Use Money

borrow money

C. Discuss your ideas from Activities A and B with a partner.

D. Circle the best answer for you. Different answers are possible.

1. Where do people in your country keep their money?

   a. in a bank

   b. in a different place

2. What percentage of people you know use banks?

   a. less than 50 percent

   b. more than 50 percent

3. How do you pay for things?

   a. Most often, I pay for things online with my computer.

   b. Most often, I pay for things with money from the bank.

4. Which is true for you?

   a. At the bank, I need to talk to a bank worker.

   b. At the bank, I use a computer or machine.

▲▲ **DURING READING**
► Vocabulary strategy: Financial collocations
► Reading strategy: Analyze charts and spreadsheets

◉ **Reading 1**

A. Think about the ideas as you read. Slow down if you need more time. Then read the text again. Now you can read faster. You can understand better.

Banks, Then and Now

Stop and Think

Read the title. How do the ideas in the first and second paragraphs connect to it?

Where do you keep your **money**? Why? About 50 percent of the adults in the world have **bank** accounts. A bank account is an agreement you have with a bank. The bank lets you keep your money there. People use banks for different reasons. They want to **save** money. They want to keep their money safe. They can get their **pay** from their job put directly into their account. Then they can make payments from their bank account. Banks also let people **borrow** money and **pay** it back later. The first banks opened for the same reasons people use them today. In fact, much of banking is the same as it was thousands of years ago. Even in the time of Julius Caesar (more than 2,000 years ago), people used banks. There was **debt**, and people borrowed and saved money. However, now banking is changing.

More and more people do their banking online. They do not go to the bank. They use cash machines to get their money. In 2014, banks closed more than 1,400 of their offices. Now banks are doing business differently. Some banks are designing a new kind of office. They want customers to go there. They are making the bank look nice. And there are no bank workers. **Customers** can deposit money and make other changes to their accounts. But these things are not done by a human worker. Instead, a computer makes these changes. What do you think? Do we need banks? What will banks be like in 50 years?

SAVINGS DEPOSIT

DATE _Jan 3, 2016_

NAME _Junyi Chen_

ACCOUNT NUMBER
9 8 8 7 7 7 6 5 4 3

	$	
CASH ►	$	50.00
CHECKS ►	$	250.00
	$	.
	$	.
SUBTOTAL ►	$	300.00
LESS CASH ►	$	60.00
TOTAL ►	$	240.00

Some people fill out forms like the one above to deposit their money in a bank. Others use cash machines or do all their banking online.

Check Your Understanding

B. The writer talks about banks in the past and now. Check the statements that were true in the past and are still true now.

1. ___✓___ People keep money safe in banks.

2. _____ People save and borrow money.

3. _____ Bank offices are nice places.

4. _____ People use banks because of debt.

5. _____ People use cash machines to get their money.

C. Circle the correct answer.

1. Which sentence supports the idea "People use banks for different reasons"?

   a. They want to keep their money safe.

   b. Now banks are doing business differently.

2. Why did banks close their offices?

   a. People do their banking online.

   b. They want people to go there.

3. Customers don't talk to a bank worker.

   a. This was true in the past.

   b. This is true now.

Vocabulary Strategy

Financial Collocations

Financial collocations are words and phrases we use to talk about money. What do we do with money? We *spend money*, *get money*, and *make money*. These verbs often appear with the word *money*. They are collocations. Recognizing collocations can help you understand the meaning of a sentence more quickly.

There are other financial collocations. For example, when you *make money*, you work for it and receive it. When you *pay money back*, you give it to the person you borrowed it from.

Another word for money is *cash*. *Cash* is coins and bills. It is not credit cards or other payments. These are collocations with *cash*:

   pay in cash   cash only   out of cash   cash machine

GO ONLINE
for more
practice

D. Complete each sentence with a collocation from the box.

cash machine	cash only	make money	pay in cash	out of cash

1. Oh, no! The restaurant is _____, and I don't have any.

2. How will you _____ in Tehran? Do you have a job there?

3. I'm sorry. I want to pay you back, but I am _____.

4. On the bus, you can only _____. They don't accept credit cards.

5. I need to find a _____ to get some cash.

Reading Strategy

Analyze Charts and Spreadsheets

Charts and spreadsheets show numerical information. Analyze charts and spreadsheets to help you understand numerical information in a text. The information is in categories. The categories are the groups of information. Charts and spreadsheets have titles.

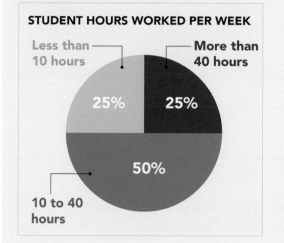

STUDENT HOURS WORKED PER WEEK

Less than 10 hours — 25%

More than 40 hours — 25%

10 to 40 hours — 50%

Pie charts show percents. A percentage is an amount of something, expressed as part of one hundred.

	A	B	C	D
1	**Earnings by Week**			
2	**Week**	**Hours Worked**	**Pay per Hour**	**Total Earnings**
3	1	15	$10	$150
4	2	25	$10	$250
5	3	12	$10	$120
6	4	15	$10	$150
7	5	20	$10	$200
8	**Total**			**$870**
9				
10				

Spreadsheets like this one show important numbers and how they add up.

GO ONLINE
for more practice

E. Answer the questions about the chart and spreadsheet in the Reading Strategy box.

1. What is the title of the spreadsheet? _____

2. What are the categories in the pie chart? _____

_____

3. What is the total in the spreadsheet? _____

Reading 2

A. Preview the text. Then read it to yourself.

How to Set a Budget

If you want to stay out of **debt**, you need to set a budget. A budget is a plan for how to **spend** your **money**. First, know what you are spending your money on. Write down what you buy and how much you spend. You can use an app or a computer program. Then look at your information. First, write how much your food, housing, transportation, and other monthly bills like electricity **cost**. These are your needs. Then write your goals. These are any debts you have to **pay** and money you want to **save**. Then write the other things you enjoy. These are extras, such as going to restaurants, movies, or the gym. These are the things you like but don't need. How much do you spend on these extras each month?

Now look at your income. Your income is the amount of money you make each month. How much of it do you spend on needs, goals, and extras? One good rule is 50 percent of your paycheck is for your needs. Pay for things in this order: needs first, goals second, and extras third. Twenty percent is for your goals. Thirty percent of your income is for extras. The first step in setting a budget is to know where your money goes. Then you can make payments, plan for your goals, and make good financial **choices**.

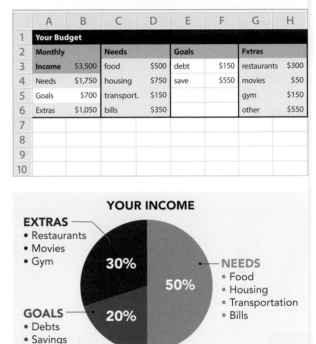

	A	B	C	D	E	F	G	H
1	Your Budget							
2	Monthly		Needs		Goals		Extras	
3	Income	$3,500	food	$500	debt	$150	restaurants	$300
4	Needs	$1,750	housing	$750	save	$550	movies	$50
5	Goals	$700	transport.	$150			gym	$150
6	Extras	$1,050	bills	$350			other	$550
7								
8								
9								
10								

YOUR INCOME

EXTRAS
- Restaurants
- Movies
- Gym

30%

50%

NEEDS
- Food
- Housing
- Transportation
- Bills

GOALS
- Debts
- Savings

20%

Grammar in the Readings

Notice *want to* + verbs in the readings.

Use *want to* + verbs to tell what you wish to do.

> They **want to** <u>save</u> money. They **want to** <u>keep</u> their money safe.

Use the present progressive to talk about things you are doing now.

> I **am paying** for my bus ride.

Notice the present progressive in the readings.

The present progressive uses a form of *be* and a verb + *-ing*.

> I **am paying**.   We **are paying**.
> He/she **is paying**.   They **are paying**.

Stop and Think

What extras do you spend money on? Are extras the same for everyone?

GO ONLINE
for grammar practice

Check Your Understanding

B. Match each item to the category it belongs in.

| debt | housing | movies | restaurants | savings | transportation |

Needs	Goals	Extras
_____ *housing* _____	_____	_____
_____	_____	_____

Recycle

the Vocabulary
Strategy

Vocabulary Strategy: Financial Collocations

C. Complete each sentence with a word from the text.

1. It is important to learn how to _____ *set* _____ a budget.

2. If you want to stay _____ of debt, you need to set a budget.

3. How much do you spend _____ these extras each month?

4. Pay _____ things in this order.

5. Then you can _____ payments, plan for your goals, and make good financial choices.

Recycle

the Reading
Strategy

Reading Strategy: Analyze Charts and Spreadsheets

D. Look at the pie chart and spreadsheet on page 127. Answer the questions.

1. How much money is saved each month? _____ *$550* _____

2. What part of the pie chart shows the smallest percentage? _____

3. How much money is spent on restaurants? _____

4. What is the monthly income? _____

5. How much debt is paid a month? _____

⬤ Make Connections: Text to Text

A. Both writers give the definition of a key word. The word is important to the text. Write the key word and its meaning.

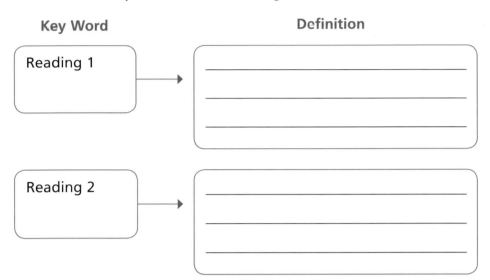

Key Word

Reading 1

Definition

Reading 2

B. Both writers use the words *want to*. Complete the sentences using words from the different texts.

1. They want to _____

2. They want to _____

3. If you want to _____

4. These are any debts you have to pay and money you want to _____

C. Both writers use financial collocations. Complete the collocations with the words from the box. Use the words in bold to help you.

payments	borrow	save	pay	for	set

People _____ **money** from banks, but they have to

_____ **back** the money. Many people **make** _____ to

the bank for years. It can take a long time to **pay** _____ a house or other

item. It helps to _____ **a budget** and _____ **money** for

things you want.

Summarizing and Retelling

A. Complete the questions and answers with the words from the box. Some of the words have to be changed to fit the sentences. For example, *bank* has to be changed to *banks*. Then read the text to a partner to retell the ideas.

Nouns	Verbs
bank	borrow
choice	cost
customer	pay
debt	save
money	spend

1. Why do people use _____?

   People use banks to _____ and _____ money.

   People also use banks to _____ for things from their account.

2. Why are banks changing?

   More and more _____ do their banking online.

3. What is the first thing to do when you set a budget?

   You need to know what you _____ your _____ on.

   You tell how much things _____.

4. What is in your budget?

   It is your _____ how much to spend on extras. These are 30 percent of your income. You also tell how much you pay for your goals. This is _____ and money you want to save.

Word Partners

big money

earn money

get money

raise money

waste money

GO ONLINE
to practice
word partners

B. Think about the question each text asks. Then give an answer to that question.

Reading 1 question:

_____

Answer: _____

_____

Reading 2 question:

_____

Answer: _____

_____

● Make Connections: Text to World

A. Complete the Venn diagram with ideas from the texts on pages 124 and 127 and your own ideas. Look at the Oxford 2000 keywords on page 133 and find three words to help you.

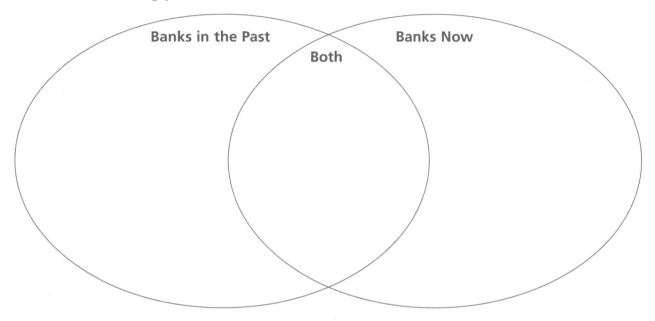

Banks in the Past   Banks Now

Both

B. Compare your answers from Activity A with a partner.

C. Look at the Extras section of the spreadsheet on page 127. Write three other choices for extras.

1. _____

2. _____

3. _____

D. Answer the questions.

1. Which text did the writer write to help people? _____

_____

2. Which text did the writer write to interest people? _____

_____

3. When do writers use a definition in the text? _____

_____

4. Will people in the future use banks? _____

_____

5. Do you agree with how to set a budget? What are some other ways to set a budget?

_____

_____

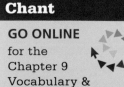

Chant

GO ONLINE
for the
Chapter 9
Vocabulary &
Grammar Chant

Look at the word bank for Unit 3. Check (✓) the words you know. Circle the words you want to learn better.

OXFORD 2000 ⚷

Adjectives	Nouns		Verbs	
medical	bank	manager	borrow	invent
possible	camera	money	cost	need
	choice	past	design	pay
	customer	research	develop	save
	debt	skill	employ	spend
	field	speed	fly	work
	job		imagine	

PRACTICE WITH THE OXFORD 2000 ⚷

A. Use the words in the chart. Match adjectives with nouns.

1. _____possible choice_____   2. _____

3. _____   4. _____

5. _____

B. Use the words in the chart. Match verbs with nouns.

1. _____borrow money_____   2. _____

3. _____   4. _____

5. _____

C. Use the words in the chart. Match verbs with adjective noun partners.

1. _____develop medical research_____   2. _____

3. _____   4. _____

5. _____

THE OXFORD 2000 ✎ LIST OF KEYWORDS

This is a list of the 2000 most important and useful words to learn at this stage in your language learning. These words have been carefully chosen by a group of language experts and experienced teachers, who have judged the words to be important and useful for three reasons.

- Words that are used very **frequently** (= very often) in English are included in this list. Frequency information has been gathered from the American English section of the Oxford English Corpus, which is a collection of written and spoken texts containing over 2 billion words.

- The keywords are frequent across a **range** of different types of text. This means that the keywords are often used in a variety of contexts, not just in newspapers or in scientific articles for example.

- The list includes some important words which are very **familiar** to most users of English, even though they are not used very frequently. These include, for example, words which are useful for explaining what you mean when you do not know the exact word for something.

Names of people, places, etc. beginning with a capital letter are not included in the list of 2000 keywords. Keywords which are not included in the list are numbers, days of the week, and the months of the year.

A

a, an *indefinite article*
ability *n.*
able *adj.*
about *adv., prep.*
above *prep., adv.*
absolutely *adv.*
academic *adj.*
accept *v.*
acceptable *adj.*
accident *n.*
  by accident
according to prep.
account *n.*
accurate *adj.*
accuse *v.*
achieve *v.*
achievement *n.*
acid *n.*
across *adv., prep.*
act *n., v.*
action *n.*
active *adj.*
activity *n.*
actor, actress *n.*
actual *adj.*
actually *adv.*
add *v.*
address *n.*
admire *v.*
admit *v.*
adult *n.*
advanced *adj.*
advantage *n.*
adventure *n.*
advertisement *n.*
advice *n.*

advise *v.*
affect *v.*
afford *v.*
afraid *adj.*
after *prep., conj., adv.*
afternoon *n.*
afterward *adv.*
again *adv.*
against *prep.*
age *n.*
  aged *adj.*
ago *adv.*
agree *v.*
agreement *n.*
ahead *adv.*
aim *n., v.*
air *n.*
airplane *n.*
airport *n.*
alarm *n.*
alcohol *n.*
alcoholic *adj.*
alive *adj.*
all *adj., pron., adv.*
allow *v.*
all right *adj., adv.,*
  exclamation
almost *adv.*
alone *adj., adv.*
along *prep., adv.*
alphabet *n.*
already *adv.*
also *adv.*
although *conj.*
always *adv.*
among *prep.*
amount *n.*

amuse *v.*
analyze *v.*
analysis *n.*
ancient *adj.*
and *conj.*
anger *n.*
angle *n.*
angry *adj.*
animal *n.*
announce *v.*
another *adj., pron.*
answer *n., v.*
any *adj., pron., adv.*
anymore *(also any more)*
  adv.
anyone *(also anybody)*
  pron.
anything *pron.*
anyway *adv.*
anywhere *adv.*
apart *adv.*
apartment *n.*
apparently *adv.*
appear *v.*
appearance *n.*
apple *n.*
apply *v.*
appointment *n.*
appreciate *v.*
appropriate *adj.*
approve *v.*
area *n.*
argue *v.*
argument *n.*
arm *n.*
army *n.*
around *adv., prep.*

arrange *v.*
arrangement *n.*
arrest *v.*
arrive *v.*
arrow *n.*
art *n.*
article *n.*
artificial *adj.*
artist *n.*
artistic *adj.*
as *prep., conj.*
ashamed *adj.*
ask *v.*
asleep *adj.*
at *prep.*
atmosphere *n.*
atom *n.*
attach *v.*
attack *n., v.*
attention *n.*
attitude *n.*
attract *v.*
attractive *adj.*
aunt *n.*
authority *n.*
available *adj.*
average *adj., n.*
avoid *v.*
awake *adj.*
aware *adj.*
away *adv.*

B

baby *n.*
back *n., adj., adv.*
backward *adv.*
bad *adj.*

badly *adv.*
bag *n.*
bake *v.*
balance *n.*
ball *n.*
band *n.*
bank *n.*
bar *n.*
base *n., v.*
baseball *n.*
basic *adj.*
basis *n.*
bath *n.*
bathroom *n.*
be *v.*
beach *n.*
bear *v.*
beard *n.*
beat *v.*
beautiful *adj.*
beauty *n.*
because *conj.*
become *v.*
bed *n.*
bedroom *n.*
beer *n.*
before *prep., conj., adv.*
begin *v.*
beginning *n.*
behave *v.*
behavior *n.*
behind *prep., adv.*
belief *n.*
believe *v.*
bell *n.*
belong *v.*
below *prep., adv.*
belt *n.*
bend *v.*
benefit *n.*
beside *prep.*
best *adj., adv., n.*
better *adj., adv.*
between *prep., adv.*
beyond *prep., adv.*
bicycle *n.*
big *adj.*
bill *n.*
bird *n.*
birth *n.*
birthday *n.*
bite *v.*
bitter *adj.*
black *adj.*
blame *v.*
block *n.*
blood *n.*
blow *v., n.*
blue *adj., n.*

board *n.*
boat *n.*
body *n.*
boil *v.*
bomb *n., v.*
bone *n.*
book *n.*
boot *n.*
border *n.*
bored *adj.*
boring *adj.*
born: be born *v.*
borrow *v.*
boss *n.*
both *adj., pron.*
bother *v.*
bottle *n.*
bottom *n.*
bowl *n.*
box *n.*
boy *n.*
boyfriend *n.*
brain *n.*
branch *n.*
brave *adj.*
bread *n.*
break *v.*
breakfast *n.*
breath *n.*
breathe *v.*
brick *n.*
bridge *n.*
brief *adj.*
bright *adj.*
bring *v.*
broken *adj.*
brother *n.*
brown *adj., n.*
brush *n., v.*
bubble *n.*
build *v.*
building *n.*
bullet *n.*
burn *v.*
burst *v.*
bury *v.*
bus *n.*
bush *n.*
business *n.*
busy *adj.*
but *conj.*
butter *n.*
button *n.*
buy *v.*
by *prep.*
bye *exclamation*

C

cabinet *n.*

cake *n.*
calculate *v.*
call *v., n.*
calm *adj.*
camera *n.*
camp *n., v.*
can *modal v., n.*
cancel *v.*
candy *n.*
capable *adj.*
capital *n.*
car *n.*
card *n.*
care *n., v.*
   take care of
   care for
career *n.*
careful *adj.*
carefully *adv.*
careless *adj.*
carelessly *adv.*
carry *v.*
case *n.*
   in case (of)
cash *n.*
cat *n.*
catch *v.*
cause *n., v.*
CD *n.*
ceiling *n.*
celebrate *v.*
cell *n.*
cell phone *n.*
cent *n.*
center *n.*
centimeter *n.*
central *adj.*
century *n.*
ceremony *n.*
certain *adj.*
certainly *adv.*
chain *n., v.*
chair *n.*
challenge *n.*
chance *n.*
change *v., n.*
character *n.*
characteristic *n.*
charge *n., v.*
charity *n.*
chase *v., n.*
cheap *adj.*
cheat *v.*
check *v., n.*
cheek *n.*
cheese *n.*
chemical *adj., n.*
chemistry *n.*
chest *n.*

chicken *n.*
chief *adj., n.*
child *n.*
childhood *n.*
chin *n.*
chocolate *n.*
choice *n.*
choose *v.*
church *n.*
cigarette *n.*
circle *n.*
citizen *n.*
city *n.*
class *n.*
clean *adj., v.*
clear *adj., v.*
clearly *adv.*
climate *n.*
climb *v.*
clock *n.*
close /kloʊs/ *adj., adv.*
close /kloʊz/ *v.*
closed *adj.*
cloth *n.*
clothes *n.*
clothing *n.*
cloud *n.*
club *n.*
coast *n.*
coat *n.*
coffee *n.*
coin *n.*
cold *adj., n.*
collect *v.*
collection *n.*
college *n.*
color *n., v.*
column *n.*
combination *n.*
combine *v.*
come *v.*
comfortable *adj.*
command *n.*
comment *n., v.*
common *adj.*
communicate *v.*
communication *n.*
community *n.*
company *n.*
compare *v.*
comparison *n.*
competition *n.*
complain *v.*
complaint *n.*
complete *adj.*
completely *adv.*
complicated *adj.*
computer *n.*
concentrate *v.*

concert *n.*
conclusion *n.*
condition *n.*
confidence *n.*
confident *adj.*
confuse *v.*
confused *adj.*
connect *v.*
connection *n.*
conscious *adj.*
consider *v.*
consist *v.*
constant *adj.*
contact *n., v.*
contain *v.*
container *n.*
continent *n.*
continue *v.*
continuous *adj.*
contract *n.*
contrast *n.*
contribute *v.*
control *n., v.*
convenient *adj.*
conversation *n.*
convince *v.*
cook *v.*
cookie *n.*
cooking *n.*
cool *adj.*
copy *n., v.*
corner *n.*
correct *adj., v.*
correctly *adv.*
cost *n., v.*
cotton *n.*
cough *v.*
could *modal v.*
count *v.*
country *n.*
county *n.*
couple *n.*
course *n.*
    of course
court *n.*
cousin *n.*
cover *v., n.*
covering *n.*
cow *n.*
crack *v.*
crash *n., v.*
crazy *adj.*
cream *n., adj.*
create *v.*
credit card *n.*
crime *n.*
criminal *adj., n.*
crisis *n.*
criticism *n.*

criticize *v.*
cross *v.*
crowd *n.*
cruel *adj.*
crush *v.*
cry *v.*
culture *n.*
cup *n.*
curly *adj.*
curve *n.*
curved *adj.*
custom *n.*
customer *n.*
cut *v., n.*

D
dad *n.*
damage *n., v.*
dance *n., v.*
dancer *n.*
danger *n.*
dangerous *adj.*
dark *adj., n.*
date *n.*
daughter *n.*
day *n.*
dead *adj.*
deal *v.*
dear *adj.*
death *n.*
debt *n.*
decide *v.*
decision *n.*
decorate *v.*
deep *adj.*
deeply *adv.*
defeat *v.*
definite *adj.*
definitely *adv.*
definition *n.*
degree *n.*
deliberately *adv.*
deliver *v.*
demand *n., v.*
dentist *n.*
deny *v.*
department *n.*
depend *v.*
depression *n.*
describe *v.*
description *n.*
desert *n.*
deserve *v.*
design *n., v.*
desk *n.*
despite *prep.*
destroy *v.*
detail *n.*
    in detail

determination *n.*
determined *adj.*
develop *v.*
development *n.*
device *n.*
diagram *n.*
dictionary *n.*
die *v.*
difference *n.*
different *adj.*
difficult *adj.*
difficulty *n.*
dig *v.*
dinner *n.*
direct *adj., adv., v.*
direction *n.*
directly *adv.*
dirt *n.*
dirty *adj.*
disadvantage *n.*
disagree *v.*
disagreement *n.*
disappear *v.*
disappoint *v.*
disaster *n.*
discover *v.*
discuss *v.*
discussion *n.*
disease *n.*
disgusting *adj.*
dish *n.*
dishonest *adj.*
disk *n.*
distance *n.*
distant *adj.*
disturb *v.*
divide *v.*
division *n.*
divorce *n., v.*
do *v., auxiliary v.*
doctor *n. (abbr.* Dr.)
document *n.*
dog *n.*
dollar *n.*
door *n.*
dot *n.*
double *adj.*
doubt *n.*
down *adv., prep.*
downstairs *adv., adj.*
downward *adv.*
draw *v.*
drawer *n.*
drawing *n*
dream *n., v.*
dress *n., v.*
drink *n., v.*
drive *v., n.*
driver *n.*

drop *v., n.*
drug *n.*
dry *adj., v.*
during *prep.*
dust *n.*
duty *n.*
DVD *n.*

E
each *adj., pron.*
each other *pron.*
ear *n.*
early *adj., adv.*
earn *v.*
earth *n.*
easily *adv.*
east *n., adj., adv.*
eastern *adj.*
easy *adj.*
eat *v.*
economic *adj.*
economy *n.*
edge *n.*
educate *v.*
education *n.*
effect *n.*
effort *n.*
e.g. *abbr.*
egg *n.*
either *adj., pron., adv.*
election *n.*
electric *adj.*
electrical *adj.*
electricity *n.*
electronic *adj.*
else *adv.*
e-mail *(also* email*) n., v.*
embarrass *v.*
embarrassed *adj.*
emergency *n.*
emotion *n.*
employ *v.*
employment *n.*
empty *adj.*
encourage *v.*
end *n., v.*
    in the end
enemy *n.*
energy *n.*
engine *n.*
enjoy *v.*
enjoyable *adj.*
enjoyment *n.*
enough *adj., pron., adv.*
enter *v.*
entertain *v.*
entertainment *n.*
enthusiasm *n.*
enthusiastic *adj.*

The Oxford 2000 List of Keywords

entrance *n.*
environment *n.*
equal *adj.*
equipment *n.*
error *n.*
escape *v.*
especially *adv.*
essential *adj.*
etc. *abbr.*
even *adv.*
evening *n.*
event *n.*
ever *adv.*
every *adj.*
everybody *pron.*
everyone *pron.*
everything *pron.*
everywhere *adv.*
evidence *n.*
evil *adj.*
exact *adj.*
exactly *adv.*
exaggerate *v.*
exam *n.*
examination *n.*
examine *v.*
example *n.*
excellent *adj.*
except *prep.*
exchange *v., n.*
excited *adj.*
excitement *n.*
exciting *adj.*
excuse *n., v.*
exercise *n.*
exist *v.*
exit *n.*
expect *v.*
expensive *adj.*
experience *n., v.*
experiment *n.*
expert *n.*
explain *v.*
explanation *n.*
explode *v.*
explore *v.*
explosion *n.*
expression *n.*
extra *adj., adv.*
extreme *adj.*
extremely *adv.*
eye *n.*

F
face *n., v.*
fact *n.*
factory *n.*
fail *v.*
failure *n.*

fair *adj.*
fall *v., n.*
false *adj.*
familiar *adj.*
family *n.*
famous *adj.*
far *adv., adj.*
farm *n.*
farmer *n.*
fashion *n.*
fashionable *adj.*
fast *adj., adv.*
fasten *v.*
fat *adj., n.*
father *n.*
fault *n.*
favor *n.*
  in favor
favorite *adj., n.*
fear *n., v.*
feather *n.*
feature *n.*
feed *v.*
feel *v.*
feeling *n.*
female *adj.*
fence *n.*
festival *n.*
few *adj., pron.*
  a few
field *n.*
fight *v., n.*
figure *n.*
file *n.*
fill *v.*
film *n.*
final *adj.*
finally *adv.*
financial *adj.*
find *v.*
  find out sth
fine *adj.*
finger *n.*
finish *v.*
fire *n., v.*
firm *n., adj.*
firmly *adv.*
first *adj., adv., n.*
  at first
fish *n.*
fit *v., adj.*
fix *v.*
fixed *adj.*
flag *n.*
flame *n.*
flash *v.*
flat *adj.*
flavor *n.*
flight *n.*

float *v.*
flood *n.*
floor *n.*
flour *n.*
flow *v.*
flower *n.*
fly *v.*
fold *v.*
follow *v.*
food *n.*
foot *n.*
football *n.*
for *prep.*
force *n., v.*
foreign *adj.*
forest *n.*
forever *adv.*
forget *v.*
forgive *v.*
fork *n.*
form *n., v.*
formal *adj.*
forward *adv.*
frame *n.*
free *adj., v., adv.*
freedom *n.*
freeze *v.*
fresh *adj.*
friend *n.*
friendly *adj.*
friendship *n.*
frighten *v.*
from *prep.*
front *n., adj.*
  in front
frozen *adj.*
fruit *n.*
fry *v.*
fuel *n.*
full *adj.*
fully *adv.*
fun *n., adj.*
funny *adj.*
fur *n.*
furniture *n.*
further *adj., adv.*
future *n., adj.*

G
gain *v.*
gallon *n.*
game *n.*
garbage *n.*
garden *n.*
gas *n.*
gate *n.*
general *adj.*
  in general
generally *adv.*

generous *adj.*
gentle *adj.*
gently *adv.*
gentleman *n.*
get *v.*
gift *n.*
girl *n.*
girlfriend *n.*
give *v.*
glass *n.*
glasses *n.*
global *adj.*
glove *n.*
go *v.*
goal *n.*
god *n.*
gold *n., adj.*
good *adj., n.*
goodbye *exclamation*
goods *n.*
govern *v.*
government *n.*
grade *n., v.*
grain *n.*
gram *n.*
grammar *n.*
grandchild *n.*
grandfather *n.*
grandmother *n.*
grandparent *n.*
grass *n.*
grateful *adj.*
gray *adj., n.*
great *adj.*
green *adj., n.*
groceries *n.*
ground *n.*
group *n.*
grow *v.*
growth *n.*
guard *n., v.*
guess *v.*
guest *n.*
guide *n.*
guilty *adj.*
gun *n.*

H
habit *n.*
hair *n.*
half *n., adj., pron., adv.*
hall *n.*
hammer *n.*
hand *n.*
handle *v., n.*
hang *v.*
happen *v.*
happiness *n.*
happy *adj.*

hard *adj., adv.*
hardly *adv.*
harm *n., v.*
harmful *adj.*
hat *n.*
hate *v., n.*
have *v.*
   have to *modal v.*
he *pron.*
head *n.*
health *n.*
healthy *adj.*
hear *v.*
heart *n.*
heat *n., v.*
heavy *adj.*
height *n.*
hello *exclamation*
help *v., n.*
helpful *adj.*
her *pron., adj.*
here *adv.*
hers *pron.*
herself *pron.*
hide *v.*
high *adj., adv.*
highly *adv.*
high school *n.*
highway *n.*
hill *n.*
him *pron.*
himself *pron.*
hire *v.*
his *adj., pron.*
history *n.*
hit *v., n.*
hold *v., n.*
hole *n.*
holiday *n.*
home *n., adv..*
honest *adj.*
hook *n.*
hope *v., n.*
horn *n.*
horse *n.*
hospital *n.*
hot *adj.*
hotel *n.*
hour *n.*
house *n.*
how *adv.*
however *adv.*
huge *adj.*
human *adj., n.*
humor *n.*
hungry *adj.*
hunt *v.*
hurry *v., n.*
hurt *v.*

husband *n.*

I
I *pron.*
ice *n.*
idea *n.*
identify *v.*
if *conj.*
ignore *v.*
illegal *adj.*
illegally *adv.*
illness *n.*
image *n.*
imagination *n.*
imagine *v.*
immediate *adj.*
immediately *adv.*
impatient *adj.*
importance *n.*
important *adj.*
impossible *adj.*
impress *v.*
impression *n.*
improve *v.*
improvement *n.*
in *prep., adv.*
inch *n.*
include *v.*
including *prep.*
increase *v., n.*
indeed *adv.*
independent *adj.*
individual *adj.*
industry *n.*
infection *n.*
influence *n.*
inform *v.*
informal *adj.*
information *n.*
injure *v.*
injury *n.*
insect *n.*
inside *prep., adv., n., adj.*
instead *adv., prep.*
instruction *n.*
instrument *n.*
insult *v., n.*
intelligent *adj.*
intend *v.*
intention *n.*
interest *n., v.*
interested *adj.*
interesting *adj.*
international *adj.*
Internet *n.*
interrupt *v.*
interview *n.*
into *prep.*
introduce *v.*

introduction *n.*
invent *v.*
investigate *v.*
invitation *n.*
invite *v.*
involve *v.*
iron *n.*
island *n.*
issue *n.*
it *pron.*
item *n.*
its *adj.*
itself *pron.*

J
jacket *n.*
jeans *n.*
jewelry *n.*
job *n.*
join *v.*
joke *n., v.*
judge *n., v.*
judgment *(also*
   judgement) *n.*
juice *n.*
jump *v.*
just *adv.*

K
keep *v.*
key *n.*
kick *v., n.*
kid *n., v.*
kill *v.*
kilogram *(also* kilo) *n.*
kilometer *n.*
kind *n., adj.*
kindness *n.*
king *n.*
kiss *v., n.*
kitchen *n.*
knee *n.*
knife *n.*
knock *v., n.*
knot *n.*
know *v.*
knowledge *n.*

L
lack *n.*
lady *n.*
lake *n.*
lamp *n.*
land *n., v.*
language *n.*
large *adj.*
last *adj., adv., n., v.*
late *adj., adv.*
later *adv.*

laugh *v.*
laundry *n.*
law *n.*
lawyer *n.*
lay *v.*
layer *n.*
lazy *adj.*
lead /lid/ *v.*
leader *n.*
leaf *n.*
lean *v.*
learn *v.*
least *adj., pron., adv.*
   at least
leather *n.*
leave *v.*
left *adj., adv., n.*
leg *n.*
legal *adj.*
legally *adv.*
lemon *n.*
lend *v.*
length *n.*
less *adj., pron., adv.*
lesson *n.*
let *v.*
letter *n.*
level *n.*
library *n.*
lid *n.*
lie *v., n.*
life *n.*
lift *v.*
light *n., adj., v.*
lightly *adv.*
like *prep., v., conj.*
likely *adj.*
limit *n., v.*
line *n.*
lip *n.*
liquid *n., adj.*
list *n., v.*
listen *v.*
liter *n.*
literature *n.*
little *adj., pron., adv.*
   a little
live /lɪv/ *v.*
living *adj.*
load *n., v.*
loan *n.*
local *adj.*
lock *v., n.*
lonely *adj.*
long *adj., adv.*
look *v., n.*
loose *adj.*
lose *v.*
loss *n.*

The Oxford 2000 List of Keywords

lost *adj.*
lot *pron., adv.*
　a lot (of)
　lots (of)
loud *adj.*
loudly *adv.*
love *n., v.*
low *adj., adv.*
luck *n.*
lucky *adj.*
lump *n.*
lunch *n.*

M
machine *n.*
magazine *n.*
magic *n., adj.*
mail *n., v.*
main *adj.*
mainly *adv.*
make *v.*
male *adj., n.*
man *n.*
manage *v.*
manager *n.*
many *adj., pron.*
map *n.*
mark *n., v.*
market *n.*
marriage *n.*
married *adj.*
marry *v.*
match *n., v.*
material *n.*
math *n.*
mathematics *n.*
matter *n., v.*
may *modal v.*
maybe *adv.*
me *pron.*
meal *n.*
mean *v.*
meaning *n.*
measure *v., n.*
measurement *n.*
meat *n.*
medical *adj.*
medicine *n.*
medium *adj.*
meet *v.*
meeting *n.*
melt *v.*
member *n.*
memory *n.*
mental *adj.*
mention *v.*
mess *n.*
message *n.*
messy *adj.*

metal *n.*
method *n.*
meter *n.*
middle *n., adj.*
midnight *n.*
might *modal v.*
mile *n.*
milk *n.*
mind *n., v.*
mine *pron.*
minute *n.*
mirror *n.*
Miss *n.*
miss *v.*
missing *adj.*
mistake *n.*
mix *v.*
mixture *n.*
model *n.*
modern *adj.*
mom *n.*
moment *n.*
money *n.*
month *n.*
mood *n.*
moon *n.*
moral *adj.*
morally *adv.*
more *adj., pron., adv.*
morning *n.*
most *adj., pron., adv.*
mostly *adv.*
mother *n.*
motorcycle *n.*
mountain *n.*
mouse *n.*
mouth *n.*
move *v., n.*
movement *n.*
movie *n.*
Mr. *abbr.*
Mrs. *abbr.*
Ms. *abbr.*
much *adj., pron., adv.*
mud *n.*
multiply *v.*
murder *n., v.*
muscle *n.*
museum *n.*
music *n.*
musical *adj.*
musician *n.*
must *modal v.*
my *adj.*
myself *pron.*
mysterious *adj.*

N
nail *n.*

name *n., v.*
narrow *adj.*
nation *n.*
national *adj.*
natural *adj.*
nature *n.*
navy *n.*
near *adj., adv., prep.*
nearby *adj., adv.*
nearly *adv.*
neat *adj.*
neatly *adv.*
necessary *adj.*
neck *n.*
need *v., n.*
needle *n.*
negative *adj.*
neighbor *n.*
neither *adj., pron., adv.*
nerve *n.*
nervous *adj.*
net *n.*
never *adv.*
new *adj.*
news *n.*
newspaper *n.*
next *adj., adv., n.*
nice *adj.*
night *n.*
no *exclamation, adj.*
nobody *pron.*
noise *n.*
noisy *adj.*
noisily *adv.*
none *pron.*
nonsense *n.*
no one *pron.*
nor *conj.*
normal *adj.*
normally *adv.*
north *n., adj., adv.*
northern *adj.*
nose *n.*
not *adv.*
note *n.*
nothing *pron.*
notice *v.*
novel *n.*
now *adv.*
nowhere *adv.*
nuclear *adj.*
number (*abbr.* No., no.) *n.*
nurse *n.*
nut *n.*

O
object *n.*
obtain *v.*
obvious *adj.*

occasion *n.*
occur *v.*
ocean *n.*
o'clock *adv.*
odd *adj.*
of *prep.*
off *adv., prep.*
offense *n.*
offer *v., n.*
office *n.*
officer *n.*
official *adj., n.*
officially *adv.*
often *adv.*
oh *exclamation*
oil *n.*
OK (*also* okay)
　exclamation, adj., adv.
old *adj.*
old-fashioned *adj.*
on *prep., adv.*
once *adv., conj.*
one *number, adj., pron.*
onion *n.*
only *adj., adv.*
onto *prep.*
open *adj., v..*
operate *v.*
operation *n.*
opinion *n.*
opportunity *n.*
opposite *adj., adv., n., prep.*
or *conj.*
orange *n., adj.*
order *n., v.*
ordinary *adj.*
organization *n.*
organize *v.*
organized *adj.*
original *adj., n.*
other *adj., pron.*
otherwise *adv.*
ought to *modal v.*
ounce *n.*
our *adj.*
ours *pron.*
ourselves *pron.*
out *adj., adv.*
out of *prep.*
outside *n., adj., prep., adv.*
oven *n.*
over *adv., prep.*
owe *v.*
own *adj., pron., v.*
owner *n.*

P
pack *v., n.*
package *n.*

page *n.*
pain *n.*
painful *adj.*
paint *n., v.*
painter *n.*
painting *n.*
pair *n.*
pale *adj.*
pan *n.*
pants *n.*
paper *n.*
parent *n.*
park *n., v.*
part *n.*
    take part (in)
particular *adj.*
particularly *adv.*
partly *adv.*
partner *n.*
party *n.*
pass *v.*
passage *n.*
passenger *n.*
passport *n.*
past *adj., n., prep., adv.*
path *n.*
patient *n., adj.*
pattern *n.*
pause *v.*
pay *v., n.*
payment *n.*
peace *n.*
peaceful *adj.*
pen *n.*
pencil *n.*
people *n.*
perfect *adj.*
perform *v.*
performance *n.*
perhaps *adv.*
period *n.*
permanent *adj.*
permission *n.*
person *n.*
personal *adj.*
personality *n.*
persuade *v.*
pet *n.*
phone *n.*
photo *n.*
photograph *n.*
phrase *n.*
physical *adj.*
physically *adv.*
piano *n.*
pick *v.*
    pick sth up
picture *n.*
piece *n.*

pig *n.*
pile *n.*
pilot *n.*
pin *n.*
pink *adj., n.*
pint *n.*
pipe *n.*
place *n., v.*
    take place
plain *adj.*
plan *n., v.*
plane *n.*
planet *n.*
plant *n., v.*
plastic *n.*
plate *n.*
play *v., n.*
player *n.*
pleasant *adj.*
please *exclamation, v.*
pleased *adj.*
pleasure *n.*
plenty *pron.*
pocket *n.*
poem *n.*
poetry *n.*
point *n., v.*
pointed *adj.*
poison *n., v.*
poisonous *adj.*
police *n.*
polite *adj.*
politely *adv.*
political *adj.*
politician *n.*
politics *n.*
pollution *n.*
pool *n.*
poor *adj.*
popular *adj.*
port *n.*
position *n.*
positive *adj.*
possibility *n.*
possible *adj.*
possibly *adv.*
post *n.*
pot *n.*
potato *n.*
pound *n.*
pour *v.*
powder *n.*
power *n.*
powerful *adj.*
practical *adj.*
practice *n., v.*
prayer *n.*
prefer *v.*
pregnant *adj.*

preparation *n.*
prepare *v.*
present *adj., n., v.*
president *n.*
press *n., v.*
pressure *n.*
pretend *v.*
pretty *adv., adj.*
prevent *v.*
previous *adj.*
price *n.*
priest *n.*
principal *n.*
print *v.*
priority *n.*
prison *n.*
prisoner *n.*
private *adj.*
prize *n.*
probable *adj.*
probably *adv.*
problem *n.*
process *n.*
produce *v.*
product *n.*
production *n.*
professional *adj.*
profit *n.*
program *n.*
progress *n.*
project *n.*
promise *v., n.*
pronunciation *n.*
proof *n.*
proper *adj.*
property *n.*
protect *v.*
protection *n.*
protest *n.*
proud *adj.*
prove *v.*
provide *v.*
public *adj., n.*
    publicly *adv.*
publish *v.*
pull *v.*
punish *v.*
punishment *n.*
pure *adj.*
purple *adj., n.*
purpose *n.*
    on purpose
push *v., n.*
put *v.*

Q
quality *n.*
quantity *n.*
quarter *n.*

queen *n.*
question *n., v.*
quick *adj.*
quickly *adv.*
quiet *adj.*
quietly *adv.*
quite *adv.*

R
race *n., v.*
radio *n.*
railroad *n.*
rain *n., v.*
raise *v.*
rare *adj.*
rarely *adv.*
rate *n.*
rather *adv.*
reach *v.*
reaction *n.*
read *v.*
ready *adj.*
real *adj.*
reality *n.*
realize *v.*
really *adv.*
reason *n.*
reasonable *adj.*
receive *v.*
recent *adj.*
recently *adv.*
recognize *v.*
recommend *v.*
record *n., v.*
recover *v.*
red *adj., n.*
reduce *v.*
refer to *v.*
refuse *v.*
region *n.*
regular *adj.*
regularly *adv.*
relation *n.*
relationship *n.*
relax *v.*
relaxed *adj.*
release *v.*
relevant *adj.*
relief *n.*
religion *n.*
religious *adj.*
rely *v.*
remain *v.*
remark *n.*
remember *v.*
remind *v.*
remove *v.*
rent *n., v.*
repair *v., n.*

The Oxford 2000 List of Keywords

repeat v.
replace v.
reply n., v.
report v., n.
reporter n.
represent v.
request n., v.
require v.
rescue v.
research n., v.
reservation n.
respect n., v.
responsibility n.
responsible adj.
rest n., v.
restaurant n.
result n., v.
return v., n.
rice n.
rich adj.
rid v.: get rid of
ride v., n.
right adj., adv., n.
ring n., v.
rise n., v.
risk n., v.
river n.
road n.
rob v.
rock n.
role n.
roll n., v.
romantic adj.
roof n.
room n.
root n.
rope n.
rough adj.
round adj.
route n.
row n.
royal adj.
rub v.
rubber n.
rude adj.
   rudely adv.
ruin v.
rule n., v.
run v., n.
rush v.

S
sad adj.
sadness n.
safe adj.
safely adv.
safety n.
sail v.
salad n.

sale n.
salt n.
same adj., pron.
sand n.
satisfaction n.
satisfied adj.
sauce n.
save v.
say v.
scale n.
scare v.
scared adj.
scary adj.
schedule n.
school n.
science n.
scientific adj.
scientist n.
scissors n.
score n., v.
scratch v., n.
screen n.
search n., v.
season n.
seat n.
second adj., adv., n.
secret adj., n.
secretary n.
secretly adv.
section n.
see v.
seed n.
seem v.
sell v.
send v.
senior adj.
sense n.
sensible adj.
sensitive adj.
sentence n.
separate adj., v.
separately adv.
series n.
serious adj.
serve v.
service n.
set n., v.
settle v.
several adj., pron.
sew v.
sex n.
sexual adj.
shade n.
shadow n.
shake v.
shame n.
shape n., v.
   shaped adj.
share v., n.

sharp adj.
she pron.
sheep n.
sheet n.
shelf n.
shell n.
shine v.
shiny adj.
ship n.
shirt n.
shock n., v.
shoe n.
shoot v.
shop v.
shopping n.
short adj.
shot n.
should modal v.
shoulder n.
shout v., n.
show v., n.
shower n.
shut v.
shy adj.
sick adj.
side n.
sight n.
sign n., v.
signal n.
silence n.
silly adj.
silver n., adj.
similar adj.
simple adj.
since prep., conj., adv.
sing v.
singer n.
single adj.
sink v.
sir n.
sister n.
sit v.
situation n.
size n.
skill n.
skin n.
skirt n.
sky n.
sleep v., n.
sleeve n.
slice n.
slide v.
slightly adv.
slip v.
slow adj.
slowly adv.
small adj.
smell v., n.
smile v., n.

smoke n., v.
smooth adj.
   smoothly adv.
snake n.
snow n., v.
so adv., conj.
soap n.
social adj.
society n.
sock n.
soft adj.
soil n.
soldier n.
solid adj., n.
solution n.
solve v.
some adj., pron.
somebody pron.
somehow adv.
someone pron.
something pron.
sometimes adv.
somewhere adv.
son n.
song n.
soon adv.
   as soon as
sore adj.
sorry adj.
sort n., v.
sound n., v.
soup n.
south n., adj., adv.
southern adj.
space n.
speak v.
speaker n.
special adj.
speech n.
speed n.
spell v.
spend v.
spice n.
spider n.
spirit n.
spoil v.
spoon n.
sport n.
spot n.
spread v.
spring n.
square adj., n.
stage n.
stair n.
stamp n.
stand v., n.
standard n., adj.
star n.
stare v.

start *v., n.*
state *n., v.*
statement *n.*
station *n.*
stay *v.*
steady *adj.*
steal *v.*
steam *n.*
step *n., v.*
stick *v., n.*
sticky *adj.*
still *adv., adj.*
stomach *n.*
stone *n.*
stop *v., n.*
store *n., v.*
storm *n.*
story *n.*
stove *n.*
straight *adv., adj.*
strange *adj.*
street *n.*
strength *n.*
stress *n.*
stretch *v.*
strict *adj.*
string *n.*
strong *adj.*
strongly *adv.*
structure *n.*
struggle *v., n.*
student *n.*
study *n., v.*
stuff *n.*
stupid *adj.*
style *n.*
subject *n.*
substance *n.*
succeed *v.*
success *n.*
successful *adj.*
successfully *adv.*
such *adj.*
  such as
suck *v.*
sudden *adj.*
suddenly *adv.*
suffer *v.*
sugar *n.*
suggest *v.*
suggestion *n.*
suit *n.*
suitable *adj.*
sum *n.*
summer *n.*
sun *n.*
supply *n.*
support *n., v.*
suppose *v.*

sure *adj., adv.*
surface *n.*
surprise *n., v.*
surprised *adj.*
surround *v.*
survive *v.*
swallow *v.*
swear *v.*
sweat *n., v.*
sweet *adj.*
swim *v.*
switch *n., v.*
symbol *n.*
system *n.*

T
table *n.*
tail *n.*
take *v.*
talk *v., n.*
tall *adj.*
tape *n.*
task *n.*
taste *n., v.*
tax *n.*
tea *n.*
teach *v.*
teacher *n.*
team *n.*
tear /tɛr/ *v.*
tear /tɪr/ *n.*
technical *adj.*
technology *n.*
telephone *n.*
television *n.*
tell *v.*
temperature *n.*
temporary *adj.*
tend *v.*
terrible *adj.*
test *n., v.*
text *n.*
than *prep., conj.*
thank *v.*
thanks *n.*
thank you *n.*
that *adj., pron., conj.*
the *definite article*
theater *n.*
their *adj.*
theirs *pron.*
them *pron.*
themselves *pron.*
then *adv.*
there *adv.*
therefore *adv.*
they *pron.*
thick *adj.*
thin *adj.*

thing *n.*
think *v.*
thirsty *adj.*
this *adj., pron.*
though *conj., adv.*
thought *n.*
thread *n.*
threat *n.*
threaten *v.*
throat *n.*
through *prep., adv.*
throw *v.*
thumb *n.*
ticket *n.*
tie *v., n.*
tight *adj., adv.*
time *n.*
tire *n.*
tired *adj.*
title *n.*
to *prep., infinitive marker*
today *adv., n.*
toe *n.*
together *adv.*
toilet *n.*
tomato *n.*
tomorrow *adv., n.*
tongue *n.*
tonight *adv., n.*
too *adv.*
tool *n.*
tooth *n.*
top *n., adj.*
topic *n.*
total *adj., n.*
totally *adv.*
touch *v., n.*
tour *n.*
tourist *n.*
toward *prep.*
towel *n.*
town *n.*
toy *n.*
track *n.*
tradition *n.*
traffic *n.*
train *n., v.*
training *n.*
translate *v.*
transparent *adj.*
transportation *n.*
trash *n.*
travel *v., n.*
treat *v.*
treatment *n.*
tree *n.*
trial *n.*
trick *n.*
trip *n., v.*

trouble *n.*
truck *n.*
true *adj.*
trust *n., v.*
truth *n.*
try *v.*
tube *n.*
tune *n.*
tunnel *n.*
turn *v., n.*
TV *n.*
twice *adv.*
twist *v.*
type *n., v.*
typical *adj.*

U
ugly *adj.*
unable *adj.*
uncle *n.*
uncomfortable *adj.*
unconscious *adj.*
under *prep., adv.*
underground *adj., adv.*
understand *v.*
underwater *adj., adv.*
underwear *n.*
unemployment *n.*
unexpected *adj.*
unexpectedly *adv.*
unfair *adj.*
unfortunately *adv.*
unfriendly *adj.*
unhappy *adj.*
uniform *n.*
union *n.*
unit *n.*
universe *n.*
university *n.*
unkind *adj.*
unknown *adj.*
unless *conj.*
unlikely *adj.*
unlucky *adj.*
unpleasant *adj.*
until *conj., prep.*
unusual *adj.*
up *adv., prep.*
upper *adj.*
upset *v., adj.*
upstairs *adv., adj.*
upward *adv.*
urgent *adj.*
us *pron.*
use *v., n.*
used *adj.*
used to *modal v.*
useful *adj.*
user *n.*

The Oxford 2000 List of Keywords

usual *adj.*
usually *adv.*

V

vacation *n.*
valley *n.*
valuable *adj.*
value *n.*
variety *n.*
various *adj.*
vary *v.*
vegetable *n.*
vehicle *n.*
very *adv.*
video *n.*
view *n.*
violence *n.*
violent *adj.*
virtually *adv.*
visit *v., n.*
visitor *n.*
voice *n.*
volume *n.*
vote *n., v.*

W

wait *v.*
wake (up) *v.*
walk *v., n.*
wall *n.*
want *v.*
war *n.*
warm *adj., v.*
warn *v.*
wash *v.*
waste *v., n., adj.*
watch *v., n.*
water *n.*
wave *n., v.*
way *n.*
we *pron.*
weak *adj.*
weakness *n.*
weapon *n.*
wear *v.*
weather *n.*
website *n.*
wedding *n.*
week *n.*
weekend *n.*
weigh *v.*
weight *n.*
welcome *v.*
well *adv., adj., exclamation*
    as well (as)
west *n., adj., adv.*
western *adj.*
wet *adj.*
what *pron., adj.*

whatever *adj., pron., adv.*
wheel *n.*
when *adv., conj.*
whenever *conj.*
where *adv., conj.*
wherever *conj.*
whether *conj.*
which *pron., adj.*
while *conj., n.*
white *adj., n.*
who *pron.*
whoever *pron.*
whole *adj., n.*
whose *adj., pron.*
why *adv.*
wide *adj.*
wife *n.*
wild *adj.*
will *modal v., n.*
win *v.*
wind /wɪnd/ *n.*
window *n.*
wine *n.*
wing *n.*
winner *n.*
winter *n.*
wire *n.*
wish *v., n.*
with *prep.*
within *prep.*
without *prep.*
woman *n.*
wonder *v.*
wonderful *adj.*
wood *n.*
wooden *adj.*
wool *n.*
word *n.*
work *v., n.*
worker *n.*
world *n.*
worried *adj.*
worry *v.*
worse *adj., adv.*
worst *adj., adv., n.*
worth *adj.*
would *modal v.*
wrap *v.*
wrist *n.*
write *v.*
writer *n.*
writing *n.*
wrong *adj., adv.*

Y

yard *n.*
year *n.*
yellow *adj., n.*
yes *exclamation*

yesterday *adv., n.*
yet *adv.*
you *pron.*
young *adj.*
your *adj.*
yours *pron.*
yourself *pron.*
youth *n.*